100 BEST

Good Housekeeping

ONE-DISH MEALS

100 BEST Good Housekeeping
ONE-DISH MEALS

HEARST BOOKS

A Division of Sterling Publishing Co., Inc.

New York

100 Best One-Dish Meals

Copyright © 2003 by Hearst Communications, Inc.

Ellen Levine	Editor in Chief
Susan Westmoreland	Food Director
Susan Deborah Goldsmith	Associate Food Director
Delia Hammock	Nutrition Director
Sharon Franke	Food Appliances Director
Richard Eisenberg	Special Projects Director
Gina Davis	Art Director

Photography Credits

Ann Stratton: pages 10, 81, 84, 136, 144, and 146. Brian Hagiwara: pages 12, 29, 37, 53, 54, 70, 95, 107, 133, 139, and 142. Mark Thomas: front cover, pages 13, 17, 23, 24, 32, 45, 48, 59, 65, 67, 96, and 119. Alan Richardson: pages 20, 62, 76, and 116. Rita Maas: pages 43, 73, and 89. Beatriz Da Costa: pages 120 and 129.

Supplemental Text by Anne Wright

Book design by Richard Oriolo

Library of Congress Cataloging-in-Publication Data
Good Housekeeping : 100 best one dish recipes.
   p. cm.
   ISBN 1-58816-217-6
   1. Entreés (Cookery) 2. Casserole cookery.
   I. Good Housekeeping Institute (New York, N.Y.)
   TX740.G55 2003
   641.8'2--dc21   2003001536

10 9 8 7 6 5 4 3 2 1

Published by Hearst Books
A Division of Sterling Publishing Company, Inc.
387 Park Avenue South, New York, NY 10016

Good Housekeeping is a trademark owned by Hearst Magazines Property, Inc., in USA, and Hearst Communications, Inc., in Canada. Hearst Books is a trademark owned by Hearst Communications, Inc.

The Good Housekeeping Cookbook Seal guarantees that the recipes in this cookbook meet the strict standards of the Good Housekeeping Institute. Every recipe has been triple-tested for ease, reliability, and great taste.

www.goodhousekeeping.com

Distributed in Canada by Sterling Publishing
c/o Canadian Manda Group, One Atlantic Avenue, Suite 105
Toronto, Ontario, Canada M6K 3E7

Distributed in Australia by Capricorn Link (Australia) Pty. Ltd.
P.O. Box 704, Windsor, NSW 2756 Australia

Printed in China

ISBN 1-58816-217-6

Contents

Foreword

Everyone loves one dish meals, and no wonder. What could be better than breaking the crust of a potpie brimming with gravy and chunks of meat? Or digging into a plate piled high with succulent stir-fried shrimp and juicy vegetables.

Now we've compiled our 100 all-time favorite recipes—the ones readers and staff ask for time and time again—into this one volume, so you can enjoy the very best of our one-dish meals.

What do all these dishes have in common? Each one is a complete meal on its own—streamlining menu planning, shopping, cooking, and cleanup.

This comprehensive collection offers many different types of one-dish meals—quick-cooking pastas, stews, tarts, down-home potpies,

Asian-inspired stir-fries, hearty sandwiches, and a wealth of crowd-pleasing casseroles. You're sure to find the perfect fit for every occasion.

In winter, when the gang's been out sledding and skiing, serve up Polenta and Sausage Casserole, an Italian specialty that's sure to stick to their ribs. In spring, why not showcase fresh seasonal vegetables in one of our easy stir-fries, such as Thai Chicken with Asparagus?

Our cool, crisp salads make for satisfying warm-weather eating, from old favorites such as Niçoise Salad to great new ideas like Couscous and Smoked-Turkey Salad. On a cool, crisp autumn afternoon what could be better for a tailgate party than Chili Potpie with Cheddar-Biscuit Crust?

With the growing interest in healthy eating in mind, we've included many low-fat recipes. We also lightened up old favorites like Chicken Shepherd's Pie and Eggplant Parmesan, trimming fat and calories but not flavor. You'll also find some wonderfully hearty meatless dishes such as Mushroom Lasagna and Vegetarian Black Bean Burritos.

While one-dish meals make great everyday fare, they are also ideal for entertaining. Why not try our Couscous Paella, Shrimp Creole, or Carbonnades à la Flamande for your next company dinner?

But the best part of this book—we think—is that every recipe has been triple-tested in the Good Housekeeping kitchens to ensure great results every time you make it. So get ready to treat your friends and family to some wonderful eating—any time of the year.

Susan Westmoreland
FOOD DIRECTOR, GOOD HOUSEKEEPING

Smoked Turkey and Mango Wraps

A Great Start

When you need dinner in a hurry, canned chicken and vegetable broth make it easy, and all of the recipes in this book will taste delicious made with broth right off your pantry shelves. But if you want a truly superlative meal, nothing beats the flavor of homemade broth. And, it's easy to make. Start the broth on a day when you have time to let it simmer for four hours. Be sure to plan your menu ahead to use the cooked chicken in a soup, sandwich, or salad. Our recipes yield fairly large amounts, which means you can freeze the broth in sturdy containers for up to three months, and it will be on hand when you need it—almost as easy as canned!

Skimming chicken broth.

Homemade Chicken Broth

⏲ PREP 10 minutes plus cooling COOK 4 hours 30 minutes MAKES 5–6 cups

In 6-quart saucepot, combine **1 chicken (3 to 3½ pounds), including neck** (giblets reserved for another use), **2 carrots**, peeled and cut into 2-inch pieces, **1 stalk celery**, cut into 2-inch pieces, **1 medium onion**, cut into quarters, **5 parsley sprigs, 1 garlic clove,** ½ **teaspoon dried thyme,** ½ **bay leaf,** and enough **water** to cover **(about 3 quarts)**; heat to boiling over high heat. Skim foam from surface. Reduce heat and simmer 1 hour, turning chicken once and skimming. Remove from heat; transfer chicken to large bowl. When cool enough to handle, remove skin and bones from chicken. (Reserve chicken for another use.) Return skin and bones to saucepot and heat to boiling. Skim foam; reduce heat and simmer 3 hours. Strain broth through colander into large bowl; discard solids. Strain again through sieve into containers; cool. Cover and refrigerate to use within 3 days, or freeze up to 4 months. To use, skim and discard fat from surface of broth.

EACH CUP About 36 calories | 3 g protein | 4 g carbohydrate | 1 g total fat (1 g saturated) | 3 mg cholesterol | 91 mg sodium.

Vegetable Broth

⏲ PREP 25 minutes COOK 2 hours MAKES about 6 cups

Cut off roots and trim dark green tops from **4 large leeks**; thinly slice leeks. Rinse leeks in large bowl of cold water, swishing to remove sand; transfer to colander to drain, leaving sand in bottom of bowl. In 6-quart saucepot, combine leeks, **2 to 4 garlic cloves**, not peeled, **1 cup water**, and **pinch salt**; heat to boiling. Reduce heat to medium; cover and cook until leeks are tender, about 15 minutes. Add **1 large all-purpose potato**, peeled, cut lengthwise in half, and thinly sliced, **1 small fennel bulb**, trimmed and chopped (optional), **3 parsnips**, peeled and thinly sliced (optional), **2 large carrots**, peeled and thinly sliced, **3 stalks celery with leaves**, thinly sliced, **4 ounces mushrooms**, trimmed and thinly sliced, **10 parsley sprigs, 4 thyme sprigs, 2 bay leaves, 1 teaspoon whole black pepper-**

corns, and **12 cups water**; heat to boiling. Reduce heat and simmer, uncovered, at least 1 hour 30 minutes. Taste and continue cooking if flavor is not concentrated enough. Season with **salt and pepper** to taste. Strain broth through fine-mesh sieve into containers, pressing on solids with back of wooden spoon to extract liquid; cool. Cover and refrigerate to use within 3 days, or freeze up to 4 months.

EACH CUP About 19 calories | 1 g protein | 4 g carbohydrate | 0 g total fat (0 g saturated) | 0 mg cholesterol | 9 mg sodium.

Better Beans

Dried beans that have been soaked and cooked are tastier than canned and yield a firmer texture. Plus, they are much lower in sodium.

Before soaking, sort through the beans to remove tiny stones or debris. Place the beans in a colander and rinse well with cold water, running your fingers through the beans to reveal any bits of dirt. Transfer the beans to a large bowl. (Dried beans rehydrate to at least double their size, so be sure to use a large bowl.) Add enough cold water to cover the beans by two inches. The standard "overnight" (about eight hours) soaking time is really for the cook's convenience. The job is done when the beans have swelled to about double their size, which takes about four hours, but beans can be soaked for up to twenty-four hours. In hot weather, to prevent the beans from fermenting, refrigerate them while they soak. If you want to reduce the soaking time by about half, cover the beans with boiling water instead of cold. Just before cooking, drain the soaked beans and rinse them again. Discard the soaking water and cook the beans in fresh water.

Quick-Soak Technique

When time is of the essence, use this fast method: Combine the beans and cold water in a pot and heat to boiling; cook for three minutes. Remove from the heat, cover tightly, and set aside for one hour; drain and rinse the beans. Although this process saves time, quick-soaked beans tend to break up during cooking. In a chili or bean stew, a few broken beans are not a problem. But if you want the beans to remain whole, for a bean salad, for example, use the long-soak method.

Cooking Dried Beans

There is an enormous range of cooking times for dried beans. Use the directions on the package as a guide, then taste often to check for doneness, because their age and relative dryness will affect the exact time.

Dried beans should always be cooked in soft water, or they will be tough. If you live in an area with hard water, add a pinch of baking soda to the cooking water. Because water boils at a lower temperature in high altitudes, beans will take longer to cook at high altitudes; be sure they are well-soaked and softened before cooking. Adding salt to beans at the beginning of cooking toughens the skin and increases the cooking time. However, beans usually taste better when seasoned early, so we often use a minimal amount of salt when the cooking begins, then add the remainder at the end.

Although the volume changes slightly with each bean variety, one cup dried beans averages two cups cooked beans. Large beans, like limas, yield about two and one-half cups, whereas small beans, such as black beans, yield just under two cups.

Ready to Go

For the best flavor we like to cook from scratch when possible. Fresh shrimp and mussels are more succulent than frozen. However, they must be properly prepared before you add them to your recipe. Here's how to do so quickly and easily. Be sure to use fresh seafood within two days of purchase.

Shelling and Deveining Shrimp

1. With kitchen shears or a small knife, cut the shrimp shell along the outer curve, just deep enough into the flesh to expose the dark vein.

2. Peel back the shell from the cut and gently separate the shell from the shrimp. Discard the shell (or use it to make fish stock).

3. Remove the vein with the tip of a small knife and discard. Rinse the shrimp under cold running water.

Scrubbing and Debearding Mussels

Scrub mussels well under cold running water. To debeard, grasp the hairlike beard with your thumb and forefinger and pull it away, or scrape it off with a knife. (Cultivated mussels usually do not have beards.)

Soups & Stews

Seafood Stew

Beef and Barley Soup

Nutty-tasting barley is often paired with lamb, but we found it tastes great when teamed up with beef. What's more, barley is rich in fiber, B vitamins, and minerals.

PREP 45 minutes **COOK** 2 hours 30 minutes **MAKES** about 16 cups or 8 main-dish servings

1 tablespoon plus 4 teaspoons vegetable oil

3 medium stalks celery, diced

1 large onion, diced

1½ pounds boneless beef chuck, cut into ½-inch pieces

½ teaspoon salt

2 cans (13¾ to 14½ ounces each) beef broth

1 can (14½ ounces) diced tomatoes

6 cups water

1 cup pearl barley

5 medium carrots (12 ounces), peeled and cut crosswise into ¼-inch-thick slices

5 medium parsnips (12 ounces), peeled and cut crosswise into ¼-inch-thick slices

2 medium turnips (8 ounces), peeled and diced

3 strips (3" by 1" each) orange peel

pinch ground cloves

1. In 8-quart Dutch oven, heat 1 tablespoon vegetable oil over medium-high heat until hot. Add celery and onion and cook until tender and golden, about 10 minutes, stirring occasionally; transfer vegetables to bowl.

2. Pat beef dry with paper towels. In same Dutch oven, heat 2 teaspoons oil over high heat until hot. Add half of beef and cook until browned on all sides. Remove to plate. Repeat with the remaining 2 teaspoons oil and the beef.

3. Return beef to Dutch oven. Stir in salt, celery mixture, beef broth, tomatoes with their juice, and water; heat to boiling over high heat. Reduce heat to low; cover and simmer 1 hour.

4. Add barley, carrots, parsnips, turnips, orange peel, and cloves; heat to boiling over high heat. Reduce heat to low; cover and simmer 50 to 60 minutes, until beef, barley, and vegetables are tender.

EACH SERVING About 320 calories | 25 g protein | 36 g carbohydrate | 9 g total fat (3 g saturated) | 41 mg cholesterol | 740 mg sodium.

Boeuf Bourguignon

Americans have come to love this French classic. It originated in the Burgundy region, which is renowned for the wonderful wine that is the basis for this robust stew.

PREP 30 minutes   **COOK** 2 hours 45 minutes   **MAKES** 6 main-dish servings

2 slices bacon, chopped

2 pounds lean boneless beef chuck, trimmed and cut into 1½-inch pieces

2 teaspoons vegetable oil

1 large onion (12 ounces), chopped

2 carrots, peeled and chopped

2 garlic cloves, finely chopped

2 tablespoons all-purpose flour

2 teaspoons tomato paste

2 cups dry red wine

½ bay leaf

1 teaspoon plus pinch salt

¼ teaspoon plus pinch ground black pepper

1 pound small white onions, peeled

3 tablespoons butter or margarine

1 teaspoon sugar

1 cup water

1 pound mushrooms, trimmed and cut into quarters if large

1. In nonreactive 5-quart Dutch oven, cook bacon over medium heat until just beginning to brown. With slotted spoon, transfer bacon to medium bowl.

2. Pat beef dry with paper towels. Add 1 teaspoon oil to Dutch oven and increase heat to medium-high. Add beef, in batches, to bacon drippings and cook until well browned, using slotted spoon to transfer beef as it is browned to bowl with bacon. Add remaining 1 teaspoon oil if necessary.

3. Reduce heat to medium. Add chopped onion, carrots, and garlic to Dutch oven; cook until onion and carrots are tender, about 8 minutes. Stir in flour; cook 1 minute. Stir in tomato paste; cook 1 minute. Add wine, bay leaf, 1 teaspoon salt, and ¼ teaspoon pepper, stirring until browned bits are loosened. Return beef and bacon to Dutch oven; heat to boiling. Reduce heat; cover and simmer until beef is very tender, about 1 hour 30 minutes. Remove bay leaf. Skim and discard fat.

4. Meanwhile, in 10-inch skillet, combine small white onions, 1 tablespoon butter, sugar, and water. Heat to boiling; cover and simmer until onions are just tender, about 10 minutes. Remove cover and cook over medium-high heat, swirling pan occasionally, until water has evaporated and onions are golden. Transfer to bowl; keep warm.

5. In same skillet, melt remaining 2 tablespoons butter over medium-high heat. Add mushrooms and remaining pinch each salt and pepper; cook, stirring, until mushrooms are tender and liquid has evaporated. Stir onions and mushrooms into stew.

EACH SERVING About 415 calories | 33 g protein | 20 g carbohydrate | 23 g total fat (9 g saturated) | 116 mg cholesterol | 261 mg sodium.

Spanish Beef Stew

Unlike most stews, this one starts with a whole piece of meat, which is shredded after cooking. A vibrant mix of bell peppers, chiles, and cinnamon gives it a distinctive flavor.

PREP 45 minutes   COOK 3 hours 30 minutes to 4 hours   MAKES 6 main-dish servings

1 beef flank steak (1¾ pounds)

1 medium onion, coarsely chopped

1 medium carrot, coarsely chopped

1 bay leaf

2 teaspoons salt

5 cups water

4 teaspoons olive oil

1 large onion, sliced

1 red pepper, cut into ½-inch strips

1 yellow pepper, cut into ½-inch strips

1 green pepper, cut into ½-inch strips

3 garlic cloves, crushed with garlic press

3 serrano or jalapeño chiles, seeded and minced

¼ teaspoon ground cinnamon

1 can (14½ to 16 ounces) tomatoes

capers for garnish

1. Cut flank steak into thirds. In 5-quart Dutch oven, heat steak, chopped onion, carrot, bay leaf, 1 teaspoon salt, and water to boiling over high heat. Reduce heat to low; cover and simmer 2½ to 3 hours, until meat is very tender. Remove Dutch oven from heat and let steak stand, uncovered, 30 minutes. (Or, cover and refrigerate overnight.)

2. In 12-inch skillet, heat olive oil over medium-high heat. Add sliced onion, peppers, and remaining 1 teaspoon salt and cook, stirring often, 15 minutes or until vegetables are tender. Stir in garlic, chiles, and cinnamon and cook 30 seconds. Stir in tomatoes with their juice; cook 5 minutes.

3. Remove beef to bowl; strain broth. Reserve 2 cups broth. (Reserve remaining broth for use another day.) With 2 forks, shred beef into fine strips.

4. Stir reserved 2 cups broth and shredded meat into pepper mixture and simmer, uncovered, stirring occasionally, 10 minutes. Sprinkle with capers to serve.

EACH SERVING About 350 calories | 38 g protein | 10 g carbohydrate | 17 g total fat (7 g saturated) | 65 mg cholesterol | 720 mg sodium.

Chinese-Spiced Beef Stew

Our new beef stew with broccoli and snow peas has a thin yet flavorful sauce accented with ginger and star anise. Try it over linguine or Chinese egg noodles.

PREP 30 minutes   COOK 2 hours to 2 hours 30 minutes   MAKES 8 main-dish servings

2 pounds boneless beef chuck, cut into 1½-inch pieces

2 tablespoons vegetable oil

⅓ cup dry sherry

2 tablespoons sugar

3 tablespoons soy sauce

1 piece fresh ginger (3" by 1"), peeled and thinly sliced

2 garlic cloves, peeled

2 whole star anise

4 strips (3" by 1" each) orange peel

3 cups water

1 bunch broccoli (1½ pounds), cut into 1½" by 1" pieces

4 ounces snow peas, trimmed

1 bunch green onions, cut into 2-inch pieces

1. Pat beef dry with paper towels. In 5-quart Dutch oven, heat 1 tablespoon vegetable oil over medium-high heat until hot. Add half of beef and cook until browned on all sides. Transfer beef to plate. Repeat with remaining oil and beef.

2. Return beef to Dutch oven. Add sherry, sugar, soy sauce, ginger, garlic, star anise, orange peel, and water; heat to boiling over high heat. Reduce heat to low; cover and simmer 1 to 1½ hours, until the meat is fork-tender.

3. With slotted spoon, transfer meat to serving bowl and keep warm. Discard star anise. Increase heat to high and boil liquid 15 minutes or until reduced to about 2 cups. Skim off fat from surface.

4. Meanwhile, in a 4-quart saucepan, heat *1 inch water* to boiling over high heat. Add broccoli. Reduce heat to low; cover and simmer 5 minutes. Add snow peas and green onions and cook, covered, about 3 minutes longer or until all vegetables are tender-crisp. Drain vegetables and add to beef mixture. Pour reduced broth on top.

EACH SERVING About 370 calories | 27 g protein | 12 g carbohydrate | 24 g total fat (8 g saturated) | 85 mg cholesterol | 460 mg sodium.

Two-Alarm Chili

A little cocoa powder helps balance the seasonings in this meaty chili. If you like really hot chili, increase the pickled jalapeño and ground red pepper to taste.

⏱ PREP 20 minutes   COOK 35 minutes   MAKES 6 main-dish servings

I tablespoon olive oil

I medium onion, chopped

2 garlic cloves, finely chopped

2 green peppers, chopped

2 pounds ground beef chuck

3 pickled jalapeño chiles, seeded and finely chopped (2 tablespoons)

3 tablespoons chili powder

2 teaspoons unsweetened cocoa

1¼ teaspoons salt

¾ teaspoon ground coriander

½ teaspoon dried oregano

¼ teaspoon ground red pepper (cayenne)

I can (14 to 16 ounces) tomatoes, chopped

1. In nonstick 12-inch skillet, heat oil over medium heat. Add onion and garlic and cook, stirring occasionally, until onion is tender, about 5 minutes. Add green peppers and cook, stirring, until tender-crisp, about 5 minutes longer.

2. Add ground beef and cook, breaking up meat with side of spoon, until meat is no longer pink. Stir in pickled jalapeños, chili powder, cocoa, salt, coriander, oregano, and ground red pepper and cook 1 minute. Add tomatoes with their juice and heat to boiling. Reduce heat and simmer chili, stirring occasionally, until slightly thickened, 15 to 20 minutes longer.

EACH SERVING About 326 calories | 33 g protein | 10 g carbohydrate | 18 g total fat (6 g saturated) | 94 mg cholesterol | 750 mg sodium.

GH Test Kitchen Tip

For extra flavor and fun, offer an assortment of toppings such as grated Cheddar, chopped black olives, diced avocado, and sour cream.

Super Bowl Chili

Our recipe for Texas-style chili contains small chunks of beef rather than ground. The classic version doesn't contain beans, but we replaced a portion of the meat with red kidney beans to cut some fat.

PREP 30 minutes   **COOK** about 2 hours   **MAKES** about 14 cups or 12 main-dish servings

2 tablespoons olive oil

2 pounds boneless beef for stew, cut into ½-inch chunks

4 garlic cloves, crushed with garlic press

2 red peppers, cut into ½-inch dice

2 jalapeño chiles, seeded and minced

1 large onion, chopped

⅓ cup chili powder

2 cans (28 ounces each) whole tomatoes in puree

1 can (6 ounces) tomato paste

¼ cup sugar

2 teaspoons salt

2 teaspoons dried oregano

2 cups water

2 cans (15 to 19 ounces each) red kidney beans, rinsed and drained

1. In 8-quart saucepot or Dutch oven, heat 1 teaspoon oil over high heat until hot. Add one-third of beef and cook until browned on all sides and liquid evaporates, 6 to 8 minutes, stirring often. With slotted spoon, transfer beef to bowl. Repeat with remaining beef, using 1 teaspoon oil per batch; set beef aside.

2. Add remaining 1 tablespoon oil to drippings in saucepot and heat over medium-high heat until hot. Stir in garlic, red peppers, jalapeños, and onion; cook until vegetables are tender, about 10 minutes, stirring occasionally. Stir in chili powder; cook 1 minute.

3. Return beef to saucepot. Stir in tomatoes with their puree, tomato paste, sugar, salt, oregano, and water, breaking up tomatoes with side of spoon; heat to boiling over high heat. Reduce heat to low; cover and simmer 1 hour and 30 minutes. Stir in beans and cook 10 to 30 minutes longer or until meat is fork-tender, stirring occasionally.

EACH SERVING About 275 calories | 25 g protein | 30 g carbohydrate | 7 g total fat (2 g saturated) | 36 mg cholesterol | 1,115 mg sodium.

Moroccan-Style Lamb with Couscous

This sweet but slightly spicy stew is served on a bed of couscous, which, like Italian pasta, is made from semolina wheat.

PREP 20 minutes **COOK** 1 hour 45 minutes **MAKES** 8 main-dish servings

2 pounds boneless lamb shoulder, trimmed and cut into 1¼-inch pieces

2 tablespoons olive oil

2 garlic cloves, finely chopped

1½ teaspoons ground cumin

1½ teaspoons ground coriander

1 large onion (12 ounces), cut into 8 wedges

1 can (14½ to 16 ounces) stewed tomatoes

1 cinnamon stick (3 inches)

1¼ teaspoons salt

¼ teaspoon ground red pepper (cayenne)

1 cup water

2 pounds sweet potatoes (3 large), peeled and cut into 2-inch pieces

2 cups couscous (Moroccan pasta)

1 can (15 to 19 ounces) garbanzo beans, rinsed and drained

1 cup dark seedless raisins

¼ cup chopped fresh cilantro

1. Pat lamb dry with paper towels. In non-reactive 5-quart Dutch oven, heat 1 tablespoon oil over medium-high heat until very hot. Add half of lamb and cook until browned, using slotted spoon to transfer meat to bowl as it is browned. Repeat with the remaining 1 tablespoon oil and the remaining lamb.

2. To drippings in Dutch oven, add garlic, cumin, and coriander; cook 30 seconds. Return lamb to Dutch oven. Stir in onion, tomatoes, cinnamon stick, salt, ground red pepper, and water; heat to boiling over high heat. Reduce heat; cover and simmer, stirring occasionally, 45 minutes. Stir in sweet potatoes; cover and simmer 30 minutes longer.

3. Meanwhile, prepare couscous as package label directs.

4. Add garbanzo beans and raisins to Dutch oven. Cover and cook, stirring once or twice, until lamb and vegetables are tender, about 5 minutes longer.

5. Just before serving, stir cilantro into stew and remove the cinnamon stick. Serve lamb stew on couscous.

EACH SERVING About 570 calories | 33 g protein | 81 g carbohydrate | 13 g total fat (3 g saturated) | 75 mg cholesterol | 651 mg sodium.

Roasted Chile and Tomatillo Stew

At New Mexico's chile stands, green chile is as popular as red. Tangy tomatillos, which look like small, firm green tomatoes covered with papery husks, are sold fresh or canned. Dark green poblano chiles are sometimes called fresh ancho chiles, but don't confuse them with dried anchos.

PREP 1 hour   BAKE 2 hours 30 minutes to 3 hours   MAKES 8 main-dish servings

4 poblano chiles or 2 green peppers

1 bunch cilantro

3 garlic cloves, minced

1½ teaspoons salt

2 pounds boneless pork shoulder, cut into ¾-inch pieces

2 medium onions, finely chopped

3 serrano or jalapeño chiles, seeded and minced

1 teaspoon ground cumin

¼ teaspoon ground red pepper (cayenne)

2 pounds tomatillos, husked, rinsed, and each cut into quarters

1 can (15¼ to 16 ounces) whole-kernel corn, drained

warm flour tortillas (optional)

1. Preheat broiler. Line broiling pan (without rack) with foil. Place poblanos or green peppers in pan and broil at closest position to source of heat, turning occasionally, until charred all over, about 15 minutes. Wrap foil around poblanos and allow to steam until cool enough to handle. Remove and discard skin and seeds; cut poblano chiles into 1-inch pieces.

2. Turn oven control to 325°F. Chop enough cilantro leaves and stems to measure ¼ cup; chop and reserve another ¼ cup cilantro leaves for garnish. On cutting board, mash garlic to a paste with salt. Transfer garlic mixture to heavy 5-quart Dutch oven with cilantro leaves and stems, pork, onions, serranos, cumin, and ground red pepper. Toss to combine. Cover and bake 1 hour.

3. Stir in tomatillos and roasted poblanos. Cover and bake 1½ to 2 hours longer, until meat is very tender. Skim fat. Stir in corn; heat through. Sprinkle with reserved cilantro and serve with tortillas if you like.

EACH SERVING WITHOUT TORTILLAS About 370 calories | 23 g protein | 20 g carbohydrate | 23 g total fat (8 g saturated) | 67 mg cholesterol | 600 mg sodium.

Latin American Pork Stew

Pork, black beans, cilantro, and sweet potatoes give this dish authentic Latino flavor.

⏱ **PREP** 30 minutes   **BAKE** 1 hour 30 minutes   **MAKES** about 10 cups or 8 main-dish servings

2 teaspoons olive oil

2 pounds boneless pork loin, cut into 1-inch pieces

1 large onion, chopped

4 garlic cloves, minced

1 can (14½ ounces) diced tomatoes

1 cup loosely packed fresh cilantro leaves and stems, chopped

1 teaspoon ground cumin

¾ teaspoon salt

½ teaspoon ground coriander

¼ teaspoon ground red pepper (cayenne)

2 cups water

3 medium sweet potatoes (1½ pounds), peeled and cut into ½-inch chunks

2 cans (15 to 19 ounces each) black beans, rinsed and drained

1. Preheat oven to 350°F. In nonstick 5-quart Dutch oven, heat olive oil over medium-high heat. Add pork in batches and cook until lightly browned, about 5 minutes per batch. Transfer pork to medium bowl.

2. Reduce heat to medium. In drippings in Dutch oven, cook onion until tender, about 10 minutes, stirring frequently. Add garlic and cook 1 minute longer.

3. Add tomatoes with their juice, cilantro, cumin, salt, coriander, ground red pepper, and water; heat to boiling over high heat. Stir in pork; cover and bake 30 minutes.

4. Stir in sweet potatoes; cover and bake 40 minutes longer or until meat and sweet potatoes are very tender. Stir in black beans; cover and bake 15 minutes longer or until heated through.

EACH SERVING About 340 calories | 36 g protein | 36 g carbohydrate | 9 g total fat (3 g saturated) | 58 mg cholesterol | 735 mg sodium.

Moroccan-Style Chicken Stew

Our quick take on a Moroccan tagine—a sumptuous meat or poultry dish with spices, olives, and raisins—uses canned beans and chicken chunks to save time.

PREP 10 minutes   **COOK** 20 minutes   **MAKES** about 8 cups or 6 main-dish servings

1 tablespoon olive oil

1 medium onion, chopped

1 tablespoon all-purpose flour

1 teaspoon ground coriander

1 teaspoon ground cumin

½ teaspoon salt

¼ teaspoon ground red pepper (cayenne)

¼ teaspoon ground cinnamon

1½ pounds skinless, boneless chicken thighs, cut into 2-inch chunks

2 garlic cloves, crushed with garlic press

1 can (28 ounces) whole tomatoes in puree

1 can (15 to 19 ounces) garbanzo beans, rinsed and drained

⅓ cup dark seedless raisins

¼ cup salad olives (chopped pimiento-stuffed olives)

1 cup water

½ cup loosely packed fresh cilantro leaves

1. In nonstick 5- to 6-quart Dutch oven, heat oil over medium heat until hot. Add onion and cook 5 minutes or until light golden brown.

2. Meanwhile, in pie plate, mix flour with coriander, cumin, salt, ground red pepper, and cinnamon. Toss chicken with flour mixture to coat evenly.

3. Add chicken to Dutch oven and cook 7 minutes or until lightly browned, turning chicken over halfway through cooking time. Add garlic and cook 1 minute.

4. Stir in tomatoes with their puree, beans, raisins, olives, and water; simmer, uncovered, 5 minutes or until chicken is cooked through, breaking up tomatoes with side of spoon. Garnish with cilantro.

EACH SERVING About 305 calories | 29 g protein | 28 g carbohydrate | 9 g total fat (2 g saturated) | 94 mg cholesterol | 890 mg sodium.

Creole Chicken Gumbo

Gumbo gets much of its rich flavor from a deeply browned roux made with a generous amount of fat. Here, we've kept the same rich flavor but cut the fat by toasting the flour in the oven.

PREP 1 hour 10 minutes   COOK 1 hour 30 minutes   MAKES 18 cups or 12 main-dish servings

⅔ cup all-purpose flour

12 large bone-in chicken thighs (about 3½ pounds), fat removed

12 ounces fully cooked andouille or kielbasa sausage, cut into ½-inch-thick slices

6 cups chicken broth

1 can (6 ounces) tomato paste

2 cups water

2 medium onions, thinly sliced

12 ounces okra, sliced, or 1 package (10 ounces) frozen cut okra, thawed

1 large yellow pepper, chopped

4 stalks celery with leaves, cut into ¼-inch-thick slices

¾ cup chopped fresh parsley

4 garlic cloves, thinly sliced

2 bay leaves

1½ teaspoons salt

1 teaspoon dried thyme

1 teaspoon ground red pepper (cayenne)

1 teaspoon ground black pepper

½ teaspoon ground allspice

1 can (14 to 16 ounces) tomatoes, drained and chopped

½ cup finely chopped green-onion tops

2 tablespoons distilled white vinegar

3 cups regular long-grain rice, cooked as label directs

1. Preheat oven to 375°F. Place flour in oven-safe 12-inch skillet. (If skillet is not oven-safe, wrap handle with double layer of foil.) Bake until flour begins to brown, about 25 minutes. Stir with wooden spoon, breaking up any lumps. Bake, stirring flour every 10 minutes, until it turns nut brown, about 35 minutes longer. Remove flour from oven and let cool. Strain flour through sieve to remove any lumps.

2. Heat nonreactive 8-quart Dutch oven over medium-high heat until very hot. Cook chicken, skin side down first, in batches, until golden brown, about 5 minutes per side. Transfer chicken pieces to large bowl as they are browned. Add sausage to Dutch oven and cook over medium heat, stirring constantly, until lightly browned, about 5 minutes. With slotted spoon, transfer sausage to bowl with chicken.

3. Reduce heat to medium-low. Gradually stir in browned flour, about 3 tablespoons at a time, and cook, stirring constantly, for 2 minutes.

4. Immediately add broth, stirring until browned bits are loosened from bottom of pan. Blend tomato paste with water and add to Dutch oven. Stir in onions, okra, yellow pepper, celery, ¼ cup parsley, garlic, bay leaves, salt, thyme, ground red pepper, black pepper, and allspice. Add sausage, chicken, and tomatoes; heat to boiling over high heat. Reduce heat and simmer until liquid has thickened, about 1 hour.

5. Add the remaining ½ cup parsley, green onions, and vinegar; heat through. Remove from heat; cover and let stand 10 minutes. Discard bay leaves. Serve gumbo in bowls over cooked rice.

EACH SERVING About 447 calories | **27 g protein** | **28 g carbohydrate** | **25 g total fat (8 g saturated)** | **107 mg cholesterol** | **1,357 mg sodium.**

GH Test Kitchen Tip

This recipe makes a generous amount of gumbo. Any leftovers can be frozen.

Chicken and Sweet-Potato Stew

Coat chicken thighs with an exotic mix of cumin and cinnamon, then simmer with beta-carotene-rich sweet potatoes in a creamy peanut-butter sauce. Delectable over brown rice.

PREP 20 minutes   COOK 45 minutes   MAKES 4 main-dish servings

4 medium bone-in chicken thighs
    (about 1½ pounds), skin removed

1 teaspoon ground cumin

¼ teaspoon ground cinnamon

1 tablespoon olive oil

3 medium sweet potatoes (about 1½ pounds),
    peeled and cut into ½-inch chunks

1 medium onion, sliced

1 can (28 ounces) whole tomatoes in juice

3 tablespoons natural peanut butter

½ teaspoon salt

¼ teaspoon crushed red pepper

2 garlic cloves, peeled

¼ cup packed fresh cilantro leaves plus
    2 tablespoons chopped cilantro leaves

1. Rub chicken thighs with cumin and cinnamon; set aside.

2. In nonstick 12-inch skillet, heat oil over medium heat. Add sweet potatoes and onion and cook until onion is tender, 12 to 15 minutes, stirring occasionally. Transfer sweet-potato mixture to plate.

3. Increase heat to medium-high. Add seasoned chicken, and cook 5 minutes or until chicken is lightly browned on both sides.

4. Meanwhile, drain tomatoes, reserving juice. Coarsely chop tomatoes and set aside. In blender at high speed or in food processor with knife blade attached, blend tomato juice, peanut butter, salt, crushed red pepper, garlic, and ¼ cup of the cilantro leaves until smooth.

5. Add sweet-potato mixture, peanut-butter sauce, and chopped tomatoes to skillet with chicken; heat to boiling over high heat. Reduce heat to low; cover and simmer 25 minutes or until juices run clear when chicken is pierced with tip of knife. To serve, sprinkle with chopped cilantro.

EACH SERVING About 410 calories | 26 g protein | 50 g carbohydrate | 12 g total fat
(2 g saturated) | 76 mg cholesterol | 725 mg sodium.

Chicken with Rosemary Dumplings

It's not hard to cook melt-in-your-mouth dumplings. Just be sure that, during cooking, the pot stays covered and that the cooking liquid never exceeds a simmer. We used chicken breasts to shorten the prep and cooking time.

PREP 15 minutes **COOK** 1 hour **MAKES** 6 main-dish servings

2 tablespoons vegetable oil

6 large bone-in chicken-breast halves (3¼ pounds), skin removed

4 large carrots, peeled and cut into 1-inch pieces

2 large stalks celery, cut into ¼-inch-thick slices

1 medium onion, finely chopped

1 cup plus 2 tablespoons all-purpose flour

2 teaspoons baking powder

1½ teaspoons chopped fresh rosemary or ½ teaspoon dried rosemary, crumbled

1 teaspoon salt

1 large egg

1½ cups milk

2 cups water

1 can (14½ ounces) low-sodium chicken broth or 1¾ cups Chicken Broth (page 9)

¼ teaspoon ground black pepper

1 package (10 ounces) frozen peas

1. In 8-quart Dutch oven, heat 1 tablespoon oil over medium-high heat until very hot. Add 3 chicken-breast halves; cook until golden brown, about 5 minutes per side. With slotted spoon, transfer chicken pieces to bowl as they are browned. Repeat with remaining chicken.

2. Add remaining 1 tablespoon oil to drippings in Dutch oven. Add carrots, celery, and onion and cook, stirring frequently, until vegetables are golden brown and tender, about 10 minutes.

3. Meanwhile, prepare dumplings: In small bowl, combine 1 cup flour, baking powder, rosemary, and ½ teaspoon salt. In cup, with fork, beat egg with ½ cup milk. Stir egg mixture into flour mixture until just blended.

4. Return chicken to Dutch oven; add water, broth, pepper, and remaining ½ teaspoon salt. Heat to boiling over high heat. Drop dumpling mixture by rounded tablespoons on top of chicken and vegetables to make 12 dumplings. Reduce heat; cover and simmer 15 minutes.

5. With slotted spoon, transfer dumplings, chicken, and vegetables to serving bowl; keep warm. Reserve broth in Dutch oven.

6. In cup, blend remaining 2 tablespoons flour with remaining 1 cup milk until smooth; stir into broth mixture. Heat to boiling over high heat; boil 1 minute to thicken slightly. Add peas and heat through. Pour sauce over chicken and dumplings.

EACH SERVING About 437 calories | 46 g protein | 38 g carbohydrate | 10 g total fat (3 g saturated) | 137 mg cholesterol | 951 mg sodium.

Hearty Chicken and Vegetable Stew

A creamy sauce coats juicy chunks of chicken and a colorful array of vegetables in a dish that's pure comfort food.

PREP 45 minutes   COOK 1 hour   MAKES 4 main-dish servings

2 medium leeks (about 4 ounces each)

1 fennel bulb (about 1 pound)

2 tablespoons olive oil

2 tablespoons butter or margarine

1 pound skinless, boneless chicken-breast halves, cut into 1½-inch pieces

8 ounces mushrooms, thickly sliced

3 medium carrots (about 8 ounces), cut into 1-inch pieces

12 ounces red potatoes, cut into 1-inch pieces

1 bay leaf

¼ teaspoon dried tarragon leaves

½ cup dry white wine

1 can (14½ ounces) chicken broth

¼ cup water

¾ cup half-and-half or light cream

3 tablespoons all-purpose flour

1 cup frozen peas, thawed

¾ teaspoon salt

1. Cut off roots and trim leaf ends of leeks; cut each leek lengthwise in half and separate leaves. Rinse well with cold running water to remove any sand. Cut leeks crosswise into ¾-inch pieces.

2. Cut root end and stalks from fennel bulb; discard. Cut the fennel bulb lengthwise into thin wedges.

3. In 5-quart Dutch oven or saucepot, heat 1 tablespoon olive oil over medium-high heat until hot. Add 1 tablespoon butter; melt. Add chicken and cook until chicken is golden and just loses its pink color throughout. With slotted spoon, transfer chicken to medium bowl.

4. To drippings in Dutch oven, add mushrooms and cook, stirring often, until golden (do not overbrown). Transfer mushrooms to bowl with chicken.

5. To Dutch oven, add remaining 1 tablespoon olive oil; heat until hot. Add remaining 1 tablespoon butter or margarine; melt. Add carrots, leeks, fennel, potatoes, bay leaf, and tarragon. Cook vegetables 10 to 15 minutes, until fennel is translucent and leeks are wilted, stirring occasionally.

6. Add wine; cook 2 minutes, stirring. Add chicken broth and water; heat to boiling over high heat. Reduce heat to low; cover and simmer 20 minutes or until vegetables are tender.

7. In cup, mix half-and-half and flour until smooth. Stir half-and-half mixture into vegetable mixture; heat to boiling over high heat. Reduce heat to medium; cook 1 minute to thicken slightly. Stir in chicken, mushrooms, peas, and salt; heat through. Discard bay leaf.

EACH SERVING About 530 calories | 37 g protein | 53 g carbohydrate | 20 g total fat (5 g saturated) | 85 mg cholesterol | 985 mg sodium.

Coq au Vin

In this perennial French favorite, chicken cooks in a rich blend of red wine, brandy, herbs, and sautéed vegetables until tender and unbelievably delicious. Serve with boiled new potatoes or over rice or noodles.

PREP 30 minutes   **COOK** 1 hour 45 minutes   **MAKES** 8 main-dish servings

2 slices bacon (about 2 ounces), chopped

2 tablespoons olive oil

3 medium carrots, cut into ¼-inch dice

2 medium stalks celery, cut into ¼-inch dice

1 bag (16 ounces) frozen pearl onions, thawed

10 ounces large mushrooms, each cut into quarters

2 garlic cloves, minced

2 chickens (about 4 pounds each), each cut into 8 pieces, skin removed

3 tablespoons tomato paste

2 strips (3" by 1" each) fresh orange peel

3 tablespoons brandy

1¾ cups dry red wine

1 cup chicken broth

¾ teaspoon salt

¼ teaspoon coarsely ground black pepper

¼ teaspoon dried thyme

1 bay leaf

2 tablespoons all-purpose flour

3 tablespoons cold water

1. In 8-quart Dutch oven, cook bacon over medium heat until browned. With slotted spoon, transfer bacon to paper towels to drain. Pour off bacon fat from Dutch oven; reserve.

2. In same Dutch oven, heat 1 teaspoon bacon fat and 2 teaspoons oil until hot. Add carrots, celery, and pearl onions and cook, stirring occasionally, 20 minutes or until vegetables are tender and golden. Transfer vegetables to medium bowl.

3. In same Dutch oven, heat 2 teaspoons bacon fat and 1 teaspoon oil over medium-high heat until hot. Add mushrooms and cook 8 minutes or until tender and browned. Add garlic and cook 1 minute, stirring. Transfer mushrooms and garlic to bowl with other vegetables.

4. Add remaining 1 tablespoon oil to Dutch oven; add half of chicken pieces and cook over medium-high heat until browned; transfer to large bowl. Repeat with remaining chicken pieces.

5. Reduce heat to medium; add tomato paste and orange peel, and cook 30 seconds, stirring. (Tomato paste will stick to bottom of pan and darken, helping to intensify the flavor of the broth.) Add brandy and cook 30 seconds, stirring.

6. Return chicken pieces and vegetables to Dutch oven. Add wine, chicken broth, salt, pepper, thyme, and bay leaf; heat to boiling over high heat. Reduce heat to low; cover and simmer 30 minutes or until juices run clear when thickest part of chicken is pierced with tip of knife.

7. Meanwhile, in cup, with fork, mix flour with cold water until blended; set aside.

8. Transfer chicken to warm serving bowl. With slotted spoon, transfer vegetables to same bowl; cover and keep warm.

9. Slowly whisk flour mixture into broth in Dutch oven; heat until mixture boils and thickens slightly, stirring frequently. Spoon broth over chicken and vegetables in bowl. Discard bay leaf. Sprinkle with reserved bacon before serving.

EACH SERVING About 325 calories | 40 g protein | 12 g carbohydrate | 12 g total fat (3 g saturated) | 122 mg cholesterol | 485 mg sodium.

Poule au Pot with Tarragon

Stewed chicken and vegetables is a favorite Sunday supper in France. Use the leftover broth as the base for a soup.

PREP 15 minutes   **COOK** 1 hour   **MAKES** 4 main-dish servings

3 medium leeks (about 1 pound)

1 chicken (3½ pounds), cut into 8 pieces

1 pound small red potatoes

1 bag (16 ounces) carrots, peeled and cut into 3-inch pieces

4 cups water

1 can (14½ ounces) chicken broth or 1¾ cups Chicken Broth (page 9)

½ teaspoon salt

¼ teaspoon dried thyme

¼ teaspoon ground black pepper

1 large sprig plus 1 tablespoon chopped fresh tarragon

1. Cut off roots and trim dark green tops from leeks; cut each leek lengthwise in half, then crosswise into 3-inch pieces. Rinse in large bowl of cold water, swishing to remove sand; transfer to colander to drain, leaving sand in bottom of bowl.

2. In 6- to 8-quart Dutch oven, combine leeks, chicken, potatoes, carrots, water, broth, salt, thyme, pepper, and tarragon sprig. Heat to boiling over high heat. Reduce heat; cover and simmer until chicken loses its pink color throughout, about 45 minutes.

3. With slotted spoon, transfer chicken and vegetables to serving bowl. Remove and discard skin from chicken. Skim and discard fat from broth. Pour 1 cup broth over chicken. Refrigerate remaining broth for another use. To serve, sprinkle chopped tarragon on top.

EACH SERVING About 472 calories | 47 g protein | 44 g carbohydrate | 11 g total fat (3 g saturated) | 127 mg cholesterol | 859 mg sodium.

Turkey Chili

This spicy potful is made with limas and white beans—just right for a simple Sunday-evening supper. Sprinkle each serving with crushed baked corn chips if you like.

🕐 **PREP** 20 minutes   **COOK** 20 minutes   **MAKES** about 6 cups or 4 main-dish servings

1 tablespoon olive oil

1 medium onion, chopped

3 garlic cloves, minced

1½ teaspoons chili powder

1 teaspoon ground cumin

1 teaspoon ground coriander

¼ teaspoon salt

¼ teaspoon coarsely ground black pepper

1 can (15 to 16 ounces) Great Northern or small white beans, rinsed and drained

1 can (14½ ounces) reduced-sodium chicken broth

1 package (10 ounces) frozen lima beans

1 can (4 to 4½ ounces) chopped mild green chiles

2 cups bite-size pieces leftover cooked turkey meat (about 8 ounces)

1 cup loosely packed fresh cilantro leaves, chopped

2 tablespoons fresh lime juice

lime wedges (optional)

1. In 5-quart Dutch oven, heat olive oil over medium heat until hot. Add onion and cook until tender, about 5 minutes, stirring often. Add garlic and cook 30 seconds. Stir in chili powder, cumin, coriander, salt, and pepper; cook 1 minute longer.

2. Meanwhile, in small bowl, mash half of Great Northern beans.

3. Add mashed beans and unmashed beans, chicken broth, frozen lima beans, green chiles, and turkey meat to mixture in Dutch oven. Heat to boiling over medium-high heat. Reduce heat to low; cover and simmer 5 minutes to blend flavors. Remove Dutch oven from heat; stir in cilantro and lime juice. Serve with lime wedges if you like.

EACH SERVING About 380 calories | 33 g protein | 45 g carbohydrate | 8 g total fat (2 g saturated) | 44 mg cholesterol | 995 mg sodium.

Bouillabaisse

Ask Provençal cooks how to make bouillabaisse and you'll get a different and passionate response every time. But as a general rule, bouillabaisse features at least three different kinds of seafood, each with a different texture. The traditional accompaniment is aïoli, a garlicky mayonnaise (recipe below), spread on toasted French bread.

🍋 PREP 1 hour COOK 1 hour MAKES 11 cups or 6 main-dish servings

3 leeks (1 pound)

2 tablespoons olive oil

1 large fennel bulb (1½ pounds), trimmed and thinly sliced

1 medium onion, chopped

2 garlic cloves, finely chopped

pinch ground red pepper (cayenne)

1 cup dry white wine

2 bottles (8 ounces each) clam juice

1 can (14 to 16 ounces) tomatoes

1 cup water

3 strips (3" by 1" each) orange peel

½ bay leaf

¾ teaspoon salt

¼ teaspoon dried thyme

⅛ teaspoon ground black pepper

Easy Aïoli (recipe follows)

1 pound monkfish, dark membrane removed, cut into 1-inch pieces

1 dozen medium mussels, scrubbed and debearded (page 11)

1 pound cod fillet, cut into 1-inch pieces

1 pound medium shrimp, shelled and deveined (page 11)

2 tablespoons chopped fresh parsley

1 loaf French bread, thinly sliced and lightly toasted

1. Cut off roots and trim dark green tops from leeks; cut each leek lengthwise in half, then crosswise into thin slices. Rinse leeks in large bowl of cold water, swishing to remove sand; transfer to colander to drain, leaving sand in bottom.

2. In nonreactive 5-quart Dutch oven, heat oil over medium heat. Add leeks, fennel, and onion; cook, stirring occasionally, until vegetables are tender, about 15 minutes. Add garlic and ground red pepper and cook 30 seconds.

3. Add wine and heat to boiling; boil 1 minute. Stir in clam juice, tomatoes with their juice, water, orange peel, bay leaf, salt, thyme, and black pepper, breaking up tomatoes with side of spoon; heat to boiling. Reduce heat and simmer 20 minutes. Discard bay leaf.

4. Meanwhile, prepare Easy Aïoli.

5. Increase heat to medium-high. Stir in monkfish; cover and cook 3 minutes. Add mussels; cover and cook 1 minute. Stir in cod and shrimp; cover and cook until mussels open and fish and shrimp are just opaque throughout, 2 to 3 minutes longer. Discard any mussels that have not opened.

6. To serve, ladle bouillabaisse into large shallow soup bowls; sprinkle with parsley. Spoon aïoli onto toasted French bread and float in bouillabaisse.

EACH SERVING WITHOUT TOAST OR EASY AÏOLI About 312 calories | 42 g protein | 17 g carbohydrate | 8 g total fat (1g saturated) | 149 mg cholesterol | 835 mg sodium.

EASY AÏOLI In 2-quart saucepan, combine **4 cups water** and **1 teaspoon salt**; heat to boiling. Add **1 head garlic,** separated into cloves (about 14 cloves) and boil until garlic has softened, about 20 minutes. Drain. When cool enough to handle, squeeze soft garlic from each clove into small bowl. In blender, puree garlic, **½ cup mayonnaise, 2 teaspoons fresh lemon juice, ½ teaspoon** Dijon mustard, ⅛ **teaspoon salt,** and ⅛ **teaspoon ground red pepper (cayenne)** until smooth. With the blender running, through hole in cover, add ¼ **cup extravirgin olive oil** in slow, steady stream and process until mixture is thick and creamy. Transfer to small bowl; cover and refrigerate up to 4 hours. Makes about ¾ cup.

Peruvian Fisherman's Soup

A true treat for seafood lovers, this is more than just a soup. It's the main course and side dish all wrapped into one wonderfully flavorful meal in a bowl.

PREP 30 minutes   **COOK** 25 minutes   **MAKES** about 11 cups or 6 main-dish servings

1 tablespoon vegetable oil

1 medium onion, finely chopped

2 garlic cloves, minced

2 serrano or jalapeño chiles, seeded and minced

1 pound red potatoes, cut into ¾-inch chunks

3 bottles (8 ounces each) clam juice

¾ teaspoon salt

⅛ teaspoon dried thyme leaves

2 cups water

1 lime

1 pound monkfish, dark membrane removed, cut into 1-inch pieces

1 pound medium shrimp, shelled and deveined, leaving tail part of shell on if you like

¼ cup chopped fresh cilantro leaves

1. In 4-quart saucepan, heat oil over medium heat until hot. Add onion and cook, stirring often, 10 minutes or until tender. Stir in garlic and chiles and cook 30 seconds. Add potatoes, clam juice, salt, thyme, and water; heat to boiling over high heat. Reduce heat to medium; cook 10 minutes.

2. Cut lime in half; cut half into wedges and set aside. Add other lime half and monkfish to soup; cover and cook 5 minutes. Stir in shrimp and cook 3 to 5 minutes longer, just until shrimp turn opaque throughout.

3. Remove lime half, squeezing juice into soup. Sprinkle soup with cilantro; serve with lime wedges.

EACH SERVING About 215 calories | 26 g protein | 16 g carbohydrate | 5 g total fat (1 g saturated) | 117 mg cholesterol | 640 mg sodium.

Seafood Stew

A sumptuous mix of mussels, shrimp, and cod.

⏱ **PREP** 10 minutes **COOK** 20 minutes **MAKES** 4 main-dish servings

1¼ pounds all-purpose potatoes, peeled and
   cut into ½-inch pieces

1 can (14½ ounces) chunky tomatoes with
   olive oil, garlic, and spices

1 can (14½ ounces) chicken broth

⅓ cup dry white wine

16 large mussels, scrubbed and debearded
   (page 11)

16 large shrimp, shelled and deveined, with
   tail part of shell left on (page 11)

1 piece cod fillet (12 ounces), cut into
   2-inch pieces

1 tablespoon chopped fresh parsley leaves

1. In 2-quart saucepan, heat potatoes and *enough water to cover* to boiling over high heat. Reduce heat to low; cover and simmer 5 to 8 minutes, until potatoes are tender. Drain.

2. Meanwhile, in 5-quart Dutch oven, heat tomatoes with their liquid, chicken broth, and wine to boiling over high heat. Add mussels; reduce heat to medium. Cover and cook mussels 3 to 5 minutes, transferring mussels to bowl as shells open (see Tip).

3. Add shrimp and cod to Dutch oven; cover and cook 3 to 5 minutes, until shrimp and cod turn opaque throughout. Add potatoes and mussels; heat through. Sprinkle with chopped parsley.

EACH SERVING About 305 calories | 35 g protein | 28 g carbohydrate | 5 g total fat (0 g saturated) | 136 mg cholesterol | 965 mg sodium.

GH Test Kitchen Tip

Discard any mussels that have not opened after cooking.

Curried Vegetable Stew

Serve over white rice for an easy and delicious vegetarian meal. For extra crunch, add a sprinkling of toasted almonds.

PREP 15 minutes   **COOK** 25 minutes   **MAKES** 4 main-dish servings

2 teaspoons olive oil

1 large sweet potato (12 ounces), peeled and cut into ½-inch pieces

1 medium onion, cut into ½-inch pieces

1 medium zucchini (8 ounces), cut into 1-inch pieces

1 small green pepper, cut into ¾-inch pieces

1½ teaspoons curry powder

1 teaspoon ground cumin

1 can (15 to 19 ounces) garbanzo beans, rinsed and drained

1 can (14½ ounces) diced tomatoes

¾ cup vegetable broth

½ teaspoon salt

1. In deep nonstick 12-inch skillet, heat oil over medium-high heat. Add sweet potato, onion, zucchini, and green pepper; cook, stirring, until vegetables are tender, 8 to 10 minutes. Add curry powder and cumin; cook 1 minute.

2. Add garbanzo beans, tomatoes with their juice, broth, and salt; heat to boiling over high heat. Reduce heat to medium-low; cover skillet and simmer until vegetables are very tender but still hold their shape, about 10 minutes longer.

EACH SERVING About 223 calories | 8 g protein | 39 g carbohydrate | 5 g total fat (0 g saturated) | 0 mg cholesterol | 790 mg sodium.

GH Test Kitchen Tip

Curry powders can range from mild to hot—use whatever type you like best.

Three-Bean Vegetarian Chili

Hearty and colorful, this chili gets a wallop of flavor from a chipotle (smoked jalapeño) chile. If you can't find chipotles, add one or two additional fresh jalapeños, with seeds for more heat. Vary the beans according to what you have on hand, as long as you have 3 cups dried in all.

🕐 **PREP** 25 minutes plus soaking beans   **COOK** 1 hour 45 minutes   **MAKES** about 10 cups or 6 main-dish servings

1 cup dry white kidney beans (cannellini), soaked and drained (page 10)

1 cup dry red kidney beans, soaked and drained (page 10)

1 cup dry black beans, soaked and drained (page 10)

1 tablespoon olive or vegetable oil

2 medium onions, chopped

3 carrots, peeled and chopped

1 stalk celery, chopped

1 red pepper, chopped

3 garlic cloves, finely chopped

1 jalapeño chile, finely chopped

2 teaspoons ground cumin

½ teaspoon ground coriander

⅛ teaspoon ground cinnamon

⅛ teaspoon ground red pepper (cayenne)

1 can (28 ounces) tomatoes in puree

1 chipotle chile in adobo (see **Tip**, page 130), finely chopped, or 1 teaspoon ground chipotle chile

2 teaspoons salt

¼ teaspoon dried oregano

2 cups water

1 package (10 ounces) frozen whole-kernel corn, thawed

½ cup chopped fresh cilantro

1. In nonreactive 5-quart Dutch oven, combine white kidney, red kidney, and black beans and *enough water to cover by 2 inches*; heat to boiling over high heat. Reduce heat; cover and simmer until beans are tender, about 1 hour. Drain beans and return to Dutch oven.

2. Meanwhile, in nonstick 10-inch skillet, heat oil over medium heat. Add onions, carrots, celery, and red pepper. Cook, stirring frequently, until carrots are tender, about 10 minutes. Stir in garlic, jalapeño, cumin, coriander, cinnamon, and ground red pepper; cook 30 seconds. Stir in tomatoes with their puree, chipotle chile, salt, and oregano, breaking up tomatoes with side of spoon. Heat to boiling; reduce heat and simmer 10 minutes, stirring several times.

3. Add tomato mixture and water to beans in Dutch oven; heat to boiling over medium-high heat. Reduce heat; cover and simmer, stirring occasionally, 15 minutes. Stir in corn and cook 5 minutes longer. Remove from heat and stir in ¼ cup cilantro. Spoon chili into bowls and sprinkle with remaining ¼ cup cilantro.

EACH SERVING About 461 calories | 25 g protein | 86 g carbohydrate | 4 g total fat (1 g saturated) | 0 mg cholesterol | 1,048 mg sodium.

Tuscan Vegetable Soup

Healthy and hearty—dust with freshly grated Parmesan cheese.

PREP 45 minutes plus soaking beans **COOK** about 1 hour 30 minutes **MAKES** about 14 cups or 6 main-dish servings

5 medium carrots

1 jumbo onion (1 pound)

8 ounces dry Great Northern beans (1⅓ cups), soaked and drained (page 10)

1 bay leaf

3 tablespoons olive oil

4 ounces pancetta or cooked ham, chopped

3 large stalks celery, coarsely chopped

1 fennel bulb (1 pound), trimmed and coarsely chopped

2 garlic cloves, finely chopped

2 cans (13¾ to 14½ ounces each) chicken broth

1 pound all-purpose potatoes (about 3 medium), peeled and cut into ½-inch pieces

1 medium head escarole (about 12 ounces), cut crosswise into ¼-inch-wide strips

½ teaspoon salt

grated Parmesan cheese (optional)

1. Cut 1 carrot crosswise in half. Coarsely chop remaining carrots; set aside. Cut onion into 4 wedges. Leave 1 wedge whole; coarsely chop remaining wedges.

2. In 4-quart saucepan, heat beans, carrot halves, onion wedge, bay leaf, and *6 cups water* to boiling over high heat. Reduce heat to low; cover and simmer 40 minutes to 1 hour, until beans are tender, stirring occasionally. Drain beans and vegetables, reserving *3 cups cooking liquid*. Discard carrot halves and onion wedge.

3. In 5-quart saucepot or Dutch oven, heat olive oil over medium-high heat. Add pancetta, celery, fennel, coarsely chopped carrot, and coarsely chopped onion; cook 15 minutes or until vegetables begin to brown, stirring occasionally. Add garlic; cook for 1 minute, stirring.

4. Stir in chicken broth, cooked beans, reserved 3 cups bean cooking liquid, potatoes, and escarole; heat to boiling over high heat. Reduce heat to low; cover and simmer 15 to 20 minutes, until all vegetables are very tender. Discard bay leaf. Stir in salt. Serve with grated Parmesan cheese if you like.

EACH SERVING WITHOUT PARMESAN CHEESE About 335 calories | 17 g protein | 48 g carbohydrate | 10 g total fat (2 g saturated) | 18 mg cholesterol | 935 mg sodium.

Casseroles & Oven Dishes

Cabbage and Bulgur Casserole

Carbonnades à la Flamande

This Belgian standard makes a hearty cold-weather dinner. It should be prepared with a full-flavored dark beer to complement the sweet onions. But in a pinch, use lager.

PREP 45 minutes   **COOK** 2 hours 30 minutes   **MAKES** 8 main-dish servings

3 tablespoons olive or vegetable oil

2 pounds onions, thinly sliced

4 slices bacon, chopped

3 pounds lean boneless beef chuck, trimmed and cut into 2-inch pieces

½ teaspoon salt

¼ teaspoon ground black pepper

3 tablespoons all-purpose flour

1 can (14½ ounces) beef broth

1 bottle (12 ounces) dark beer (not stout)

½ teaspoon dried thyme

1 bay leaf

1. Preheat oven to 350° F. In 5-quart Dutch oven, heat 2 tablespoons oil over medium-high heat. Add onions and cook until tender and browned, 20 to 25 minutes. Transfer onions to large bowl.

2. In Dutch oven, cook bacon over medium heat until browned; with slotted spoon, transfer to bowl with onions.

3. Pat beef dry with paper towels; sprinkle with salt and pepper. Add half of beef to bacon drippings in Dutch oven and cook over high heat until well browned, using slotted spoon to transfer beef as it is browned to bowl with bacon. Repeat with remaining beef.

4. Reduce heat to medium-high. Add remaining 1 tablespoon oil to Dutch oven. Stir in flour until well blended and cook, stirring constantly, until flour browns. Gradually stir in broth and beer. Cook, stirring constantly, until sauce has thickened and boils.

5. Return beef mixture to Dutch oven; add thyme and bay leaf. Cover and place in oven. Bake until meat is tender, about 2 hours 30 minutes. Skim and discard fat from stew liquid; discard bay leaf.

EACH SERVING About 369 calories | 29 g protein | 14 g carbohydrate | 22 g total fat (7 g saturated) | 93 mg cholesterol | 574 mg sodium.

Greek Eggplant and Lamb Casserole

We roast the eggplant, rather than sauté it in the traditional way, to make a moussaka that is lower in fat and calories than usual. If you like, substitute ground beef for the lamb.

PREP 55 minutes   BAKE 35 minutes   MAKES 10 main-dish servings

2 small eggplants (about 1¼ pounds each), cut lengthwise into ½-inch-thick slices

3 tablespoons olive oil

2 pounds ground lamb

1 large onion (12 ounces), chopped

2 garlic cloves, finely chopped

1½ teaspoons salt

1 teaspoon ground cumin

½ teaspoon ground cinnamon

½ teaspoon coarsely ground black pepper

1 can (28 ounces) plum tomatoes in puree

4 large eggs

⅓ cup all-purpose flour

3 cups milk

¼ teaspoon ground nutmeg

1. Preheat oven to 450°F. Grease the 2 small cookie sheets. Place eggplant slices on cookie sheets; brush with 2 tablespoons oil. Bake eggplant until soft and browned, about 20 minutes, rotating cookie sheets between upper and lower oven racks halfway through baking time. Remove eggplant from oven; turn oven control to 375°F.

2. Meanwhile, in nonstick 12-inch skillet at least 2 inches deep, combine ground lamb, onion, and garlic and cook over medium-high heat, stirring, until lamb is browned, about 15 minutes. Skim and discard fat. Stir in 1 teaspoon salt, cumin, cinnamon, and ¼ teaspoon pepper; cook 1 minute longer. Remove skillet from heat; add tomatoes with their puree, breaking them up with side of spoon. Set aside.

3. Break eggs into small bowl and, with wire whisk, lightly beat; set aside. In 3-quart saucepan, heat remaining 1 tablespoon oil over medium heat. Whisk in flour and cook, whisking, 1 minute (mixture will appear dry and crumbly). Gradually whisk in milk. Heat to boiling; cook until mixture has thickened, about 8 minutes. Remove from heat. Gradually beat one-fourth of milk mixture into eggs. Return egg mixture to saucepan, beating to combine. Stir in nutmeg, remaining ½ teaspoon salt, and remaining ¼ teaspoon black pepper.

4. In shallow 4-quart casserole or 13" by 9" baking dish, arrange half of eggplant slices, overlapping slices to fit if necessary; top with half of meat mixture. Repeat with remaining eggplant slices and meat mixture. Pour egg mixture over top. Bake until top is puffed and golden and casserole is heated through, 35 to 40 minutes.

EACH SERVING About 375 calories | 23 g protein | 1 g carbohydrate | 22 g total fat (8 g saturated) | 157 mg cholesterol | 593 mg sodium.

Polenta and Sausage Casserole

Layers of creamy polenta, two cheeses, and a sausage-tomato sauce makes this a terrific casserole for a potluck party, buffet, or brunch. The tomato-sausage sauce is also terrific on its own, served over pasta.

PREP 1 hour BAKE 35 minutes MAKES 8 main-dish servings

8 ounces sweet Italian-sausage links, casings removed

8 ounces hot Italian-sausage links, casings removed

1 tablespoon olive oil

1 large onion (12 ounces), chopped

1 large stalk celery, chopped

1 carrot, peeled and chopped

1 can (28 ounces) plum tomatoes in puree

2 cups yellow cornmeal

1 can (14½ ounces) chicken broth or 1¾ cups Chicken Broth (page 9)

¾ teaspoon salt

4½ cups boiling water

½ cup freshly grated Parmesan cheese

8 ounces Fontina or mozzarella cheese, shredded (2 cups)

1. Prepare tomato-sausage sauce: In nonreactive 5-quart Dutch oven, cook sweet and hot sausage meat over medium-high heat, breaking up meat with side of spoon, until browned. With slotted spoon, transfer meat to bowl. Discard fat from Dutch oven.

2. Add oil to Dutch oven. Add onion, celery, and carrot and cook over medium-high heat until browned. Stir in sausage and tomatoes with their puree, breaking up tomatoes with side of spoon. Heat to boiling over high heat. Reduce heat; cover Dutch oven and simmer 10 minutes. Remove cover and simmer 10 minutes longer.

3. Preheat oven to 350°F. Prepare polenta: In 4-quart saucepan with wire whisk, mix cornmeal, broth, and salt. Over medium-high heat, add boiling water and cook, whisking constantly, until mixture has thickened, about 5 minutes. Whisk in Parmesan.

4. Grease 13" by 9" baking dish. Evenly spread half of polenta mixture in baking dish; top with half of tomato-sausage sauce, then half of Fontina. Repeat with remaining polenta mixture and sauce.

5. Bake casserole 15 minutes. Sprinkle with remaining Fontina; bake until mixture is bubbling and cheese is golden, about 20 minutes longer. Let stand 15 minutes for easier serving.

EACH SERVING About 466 calories | 23 g protein | 38 g carbohydrate | 25 g total fat (11 g saturated) | 70 mg cholesterol | 1,323 mg sodium.

Choucroute Garni

For sauerkraut lovers! This homey dish, best made in the cold winter months, hails from the Alsace region in eastern France, where the cuisine reflects the influence of neighboring Germany. Serve it with boiled potatoes, crusty bread, and a pot of good mustard.

PREP 20 minutes   **COOK** 50 minutes   **MAKES** 6 main-dish servings

4 slices bacon, cut into 1-inch pieces

¼ cup water

1 large onion (12 ounces), thinly sliced

2 McIntosh apples, each peeled, cored, cut into quarters, and thinly sliced

2 bags (16 ounces each) sauerkraut, rinsed and drained

1½ cups fruity white wine, such as Riesling

6 juniper berries, crushed

1 bay leaf

6 smoked pork chops, ½ inch thick (4 ounces each)

1 pound kielbasa (smoked Polish sausage), cut into 1½-inch pieces

1. In nonreactive 5-quart Dutch oven, combine bacon and water; cook over medium-low heat until bacon is lightly crisped, about 4 minutes. Add onion and cook, stirring frequently, until onion is tender and golden, about 7 minutes.

2. Add apples and cook until tender, about 3 minutes. Stir in sauerkraut, wine, juniper berries, and bay leaf and heat to boiling. Reduce heat; cover and simmer 15 minutes.

3. Nestle pork chops and kielbasa into sauerkraut mixture; cover and cook until pork chops and sausage are heated through and sauerkraut is tender, about 20 minutes. Remove bay leaf and serve.

EACH SERVING About 524 calories | 27 g protein | 19 g carbohydrate | 37 g total fat (13 g saturated) | 106 mg cholesterol | 3,151 mg sodium.

Indian Chicken & Rice Casserole

This dish is usually made with lamb; our lighter recipe calls for skinless chicken breasts.

PREP 30 minutes BAKE 35 minutes MAKES 6 servings

1 can (14½ ounces) chicken broth or 1¾ cups homemade (page 9)

1 cup basmati rice

3 garlic cloves, peeled

1 piece (1" by ½") fresh ginger, peeled and coarsely chopped

¼ cup sweetened flaked coconut

1 large onion, halved and thinly sliced

3 teaspoons vegetable oil

1 small red pepper, cut into ½-inch pieces

1 pound skinless, boneless chicken-breast halves, cut into ½-inch pieces

¾ teaspoon ground cumin

¾ teaspoon ground coriander

½ teaspoon salt

⅛ teaspoon ground red pepper (cayenne)

2 cups cauliflower flowerets (about ½ medium head), cut into ½-inch pieces

1 package (10 ounces) frozen peas and carrots

1 can (14½ ounces) diced tomatoes

1 container (8 ounces) plain nonfat yogurt

Raisins, toasted sliced almonds, and toasted sweetened flaked coconut for garnish (optional)

1. Preheat oven to 350°F. In 2-cup measuring cup, add *enough water* to chicken broth to equal 2 cups liquid. In 2-quart saucepan, heat chicken-broth mixture to boiling over high heat. Place rice in shallow 2½-quart casserole; stir in boiling broth mixture. Cover casserole tightly and bake 20 minutes or until rice is tender and all liquid is absorbed. Remove casserole from oven; set aside.

2. Meanwhile, in food processor, with knife blade attached, or in blender, at medium speed, blend garlic, ginger, coconut, and half of onion slices until a paste forms; set aside.

3. In nonstick 12-inch skillet, heat 2 teaspoons vegetable oil over medium heat. Add red pepper and remaining onion slices, and cook until golden, about 10 minutes. With slotted spoon, transfer vegetables to a bowl.

4. Add garlic mixture to same skillet and cook 8 to 10 minutes or until golden. Add chicken pieces and remaining 1 teaspoon oil and cook, stirring occasionally, until chicken is lightly browned on the outside and loses its pink color on the inside. Add cumin, coriander, salt, and ground red pepper and cook 2 minutes longer. Transfer chicken mixture to bowl with vegetables.

5. To same skillet, add cauliflower and *¾ cup water*; heat to boiling over high heat. Reduce heat to low; cover and simmer 6 minutes. Add frozen peas and carrots, and tomatoes with their juice; heat to boiling over high heat. Reduce heat to low; uncover and cook 2 minutes longer or until cauliflower is tender and peas and carrots are heated through. Transfer cauliflower mixture to bowl with chicken. Stir in yogurt until well mixed.

6. With fork, fluff rice. Top cooked rice with chicken mixture. Bake, uncovered, 15 minutes longer or until heated through. Serve garnished with raisins, toasted almonds, and toasted coconut if you like.

EACH SERVING WITHOUT GARNISHES About 335 calories | 28 g protein | 45 g carbohydrate | 6 g total fat (2 g saturated) | 45 mg cholesterol | 760 mg sodium.

Chicken Shepherd's Pie

Shepherd's pie was originally created as a way to utilize Sunday's leftovers. We've lightened the filling and topped it off with a mantle of creamy, chive-flecked mashed potatoes.

PREP 45 minutes   BAKE 20 minutes   MAKES 6 main-dish servings

2 pounds all-purpose potatoes (6 medium), peeled and cut into 1-inch pieces

2 tablespoons vegetable oil

2 carrots, peeled and finely chopped

1 large onion (12 ounces), finely chopped

1 large red pepper, finely chopped

2 tablespoons butter or margarine

1 teaspoon salt

¾ cup milk

2 tablespoons chopped fresh chives or green onion tops

10 ounces mushrooms, trimmed and thickly sliced

1¼ cups chicken broth

1 tablespoon all-purpose flour

1½ pounds ground chicken meat

¼ teaspoon coarsely ground black pepper

¼ teaspoon dried thyme

2 tablespoons ketchup

1 tablespoon Worcestershire sauce

1. In 3-quart saucepan, combine potatoes and *enough water to cover*; heat to boiling over high heat. Reduce heat; cover and simmer until potatoes are tender, about 15 minutes.

2. Meanwhile, in 12-inch skillet, heat 1 tablespoon oil over medium-high heat. Add carrots and cook 5 minutes. Add onion and red pepper and cook, stirring occasionally, until vegetables are tender and lightly browned, about 10 minutes longer. With slotted spoon, transfer vegetables to bowl.

3. When potatoes are tender, drain. Mash potatoes in saucepan with butter and ½ teaspoon salt. Gradually add milk; mash until mixture is smooth and well blended. Stir in chives; set aside.

4. In same skillet, heat remaining 1 tablespoon oil over medium-high heat. Add mushrooms and cook until well browned, about 10 minutes. Transfer to bowl with vegetables.

5. In 2-cup measuring cup, blend broth and flour until smooth; set aside.

6. Preheat oven to 400°F. In same skillet, cook ground chicken, black pepper, thyme, and remaining ½ teaspoon salt over high heat, stirring occasionally, until chicken is lightly browned and any liquid in skillet has evaporated, 7 to 10 minutes. Stir in ketchup, Worcestershire, cooked vegetables, and broth mixture. Cook, stirring constantly, until liquid has thickened and boils, 3 to 5 minutes.

7. Spoon mixture into a shallow 2-quart casserole; top with mashed potatoes. Place casserole on foil-lined cookie sheet to catch any overflow during baking. Bake until the potato topping is lightly browned, for 20 to 25 minutes.

EACH SERVING About 415 calories | 26 g protein | 33 g carbohydrate | 20 g total fat (6 g saturated) | 109 mg cholesterol | 848 mg sodium.

Country Captain Casserole

Though the exact origin of this well-known dish is often debated, its great flavor is never in dispute. Try it with basmati rice.

PREP 30 minutes   **BAKE** 1 hour   **MAKES** 8 main-dish servings

2 tablespoons plus 1 teaspoon vegetable oil

2 chickens (3½ pounds each), each cut into 8 pieces and skin removed from all but wings

2 medium onions, chopped

1 large Granny Smith apple, peeled, cored, and chopped

1 large green pepper, chopped

3 large garlic cloves, finely chopped

1 tablespoon grated, peeled fresh ginger

3 tablespoons curry powder

½ teaspoon coarsely ground black pepper

¼ teaspoon ground cumin

1 can (28 ounces) plum tomatoes in puree

1 can (14½ ounces) chicken broth or 1¾ cups Chicken Broth (page 9)

½ cup dark seedless raisins

1 teaspoon salt

¼ cup chopped fresh parsley

1. In nonreactive 8-quart Dutch oven, heat 2 tablespoons oil over medium-high heat until very hot. Add chicken, in batches, and cook until golden brown, about 5 minutes per side. With slotted spoon, transfer chicken pieces to bowl as they are browned.

2. Preheat oven to 350°F. In same Dutch oven, heat remaining 1 teaspoon oil over medium-high heat. Add onions, apple, green pepper, garlic, and ginger; cook, stirring frequently, 2 minutes. Reduce heat to medium; cover and cook 5 minutes longer.

3. Stir in curry powder, black pepper, and cumin; cook 1 minute. Add tomatoes with their puree, broth, raisins, salt, and chicken pieces. Heat to boiling over high heat; boil 1 minute. Cover and place in oven. Bake 1 hour. Sprinkle with parsley.

EACH SERVING About 347 calories | 43 g protein | 19 g carbohydrate | 11 g total fat (2 g saturated) | 133 mg cholesterol | 825 mg sodium.

Mustard-Dill Salmon with Herbed Potatoes

This elegant dish is surprisingly simple to make. While the potatoes cook, you can broil the salmon and whip up the no-cook sauce. For a colorful and healthy side dish, sauté snow peas in a nonstick skillet with a teaspoon of vegetable oil.

PREP 20 minutes   **BROIL** 8 to 10 minutes   **MAKES** 4 main-dish servings

12 ounces small red potatoes, cut into 1-inch chunks

12 ounces small white potatoes, cut into 1-inch chunks

1½ teaspoons salt

3 tablespoons chopped fresh dill

½ teaspoon coarsely ground black pepper

4 pieces salmon fillet (about 6 ounces each)

2 tablespoons light mayonnaise

1 tablespoon white wine vinegar

2 teaspoons Dijon mustard

¾ teaspoon sugar

1. In 3-quart saucepan, place the potatoes, 1 teaspoon salt, and *enough water to cover*; heat to boiling over high heat. Reduce heat to low; cover and simmer 15 minutes or until potatoes are fork-tender. Drain potatoes and toss with 1 tablespoon dill, ¼ teaspoon salt, and ¼ teaspoon coarsely ground black pepper; keep potatoes warm.

2. Meanwhile, preheat broiler. Grease rack in broiling pan. Place salmon on rack; sprinkle with ⅛ teaspoon of the salt and ⅛ teaspoon coarsely ground black pepper. Broil salmon at closest position to source of heat 8 to 10 minutes, until fish flakes easily.

3. While salmon is broiling, prepare sauce: In small bowl, mix mayonnaise, vinegar, mustard, sugar, remaining 2 tablespoons dill, ⅛ teaspoon salt, and ⅛ teaspoon pepper.

4. Serve salmon with sauce and potatoes.

EACH SERVING About 335 calories | 37 g protein | 31 g carbohydrate | 7 g total fat (1 g saturated) | 86 mg cholesterol | 655 mg sodium.

Shrimp Creole

A New Orleans classic, Shrimp Creole makes a good company as well as a family dish. Serve it with corn bread on the side.

🕐 **PREP** 45 minutes   **BAKE** 30 minutes   **MAKES** 6 main-dish servings

1 tablespoon olive oil

1 large onion, diced

1 medium green pepper, coarsely chopped

1 medium red pepper, coarsely chopped

8 ounces ready-to-eat chorizo sausage or pepperoni, cut into ¼-inch-thick slices

2 garlic cloves, minced

1½ cups parboiled rice

1 can (14½ ounces) stewed tomatoes

1 bottle (8 ounces) clam juice

1¼ cups water

1 package (10 ounces) frozen whole okra, thawed

1 pound medium shrimp, shelled and deveined

1. Preheat oven to 350°F. In 3- to 3½-quart Dutch oven, heat oil over medium heat until hot. Add onion and peppers and cook 10 minutes or until tender and lightly browned. Add chorizo and garlic and cook 5 minutes longer or until chorizo is lightly browned.

2. Stir in rice, stewed tomatoes, clam juice, and water; heat to boiling over high heat. Cover Dutch oven, place in oven, and bake 20 minutes. Stir okra and shrimp into rice mixture; cover and bake 10 minutes longer or until rice and shrimp are tender

EACH SERVING About 405 calories | 26 g protein | 34 g carbohydrate | 18 g total fat (6 g saturated) | 127 mg cholesterol | 800 mg sodium.

> ### GH Test Kitchen Tip
>
> Parboiled rice, sometimes called "converted" rice, is put through a steam-pressure process that results in fluffy, separate grains.

Veggie Enchiladas

Fresh cilantro gives this hearty casserole real southwestern flavor.

PREP 25 minutes   **BAKE** 20 minutes   **MAKES** 6 main-dish servings

2 teaspoons olive oil

I small zucchini (8 ounces), cut into
½-inch pieces

I medium onion, chopped

I medium red pepper, chopped

2 cans (15 to 19 ounces each) no-salt-added
white kidney beans (cannellini), rinsed
and drained

½ cup vegetable broth or chicken broth

2 garlic cloves, minced

I can (15¼ ounces) no-salt-added whole-
kernel corn, drained

2 pickled jalapeño chiles, minced, with seeds

I cup loosely packed fresh cilantro leaves
and stems, chopped

6 flour tortillas (8-inch diameter)

I jar (15½ ounces) mild salsa

⅓ cup shredded Monterey Jack cheese

lime wedges for garnish

I. In nonstick 12-inch skillet, heat olive oil over medium heat. Add zucchini, onion, and red pepper and cook until the vegetables are tender and golden, about 10 to 15 minutes, stirring frequently.

2. Meanwhile, in food processor with knife blade attached or in blender at medium speed, blend half of white kidney beans with broth until almost smooth. Transfer bean mixture to large bowl; stir in remaining beans and set aside.

3. To vegetables in skillet, add garlic and cook 1 minute longer. Stir in corn and jalapeños; cook 2 minutes longer. Transfer vegetable mixture to bowl with beans; stir in cilantro until mixed.

4. Preheat oven to 375°F. Spoon about ¾ cup bean mixture along center of each tortilla. Fold sides of tortilla over filling, overlapping them slightly.

5. Spoon ½ cup salsa into bottom of 13" by 9" glass or ceramic baking dish. Place enchiladas, seam side down, on top of salsa. Spoon remaining salsa over enchiladas; sprinkle with cheese. Bake 20 minutes. Serve with lime wedges.

EACH SERVING About 415 calories | 17 g protein | 70 g carbohydrate | 8 g total fat (2 g saturated) | 6 mg cholesterol | 700 mg sodium.

Asparagus and Green Onion Frittata

Everyone loves a skillet omelet, especially when it's filled with bits of cream cheese and sautéed vegetables. As with all Italian-style omelets, you don't have to flip this one—it's finished in the oven and practically foolproof.

PREP 25 minutes **COOK** about 10 minutes **MAKES** 4 main-dish servings

8 large eggs

½ cup whole milk

⅛ teaspoon ground black pepper

¾ teaspoon salt

12 ounces asparagus, trimmed

1 tablespoon butter or margarine

1 bunch green onions, chopped

2 ounces light cream cheese (Neufchâtel)

1. Preheat oven to 375°F. In medium bowl, with wire whisk, mix eggs, milk, pepper, and ½ teaspoon salt; set aside. If using thin asparagus, cut stalks crosswise in half; if using medium asparagus, cut stalks into 1-inch pieces.

2. In nonstick 10-inch skillet with oven-safe handle (or wrap handle with double thickness of heavy-duty foil for baking in oven later), melt butter or margarine over medium heat. Add asparagus and remaining ¼ teaspoon salt and cook 4 minutes for thin stalks or 6 minutes for medium-size stalks, stirring often. Stir in green onions and cook 2 to 3 minutes longer or until vegetables are tender, stirring occasionally.

3. Reduce heat to medium-low. Pour egg mixture over vegetables in skillet; drop scant teaspoonfuls of cream cheese on top of egg mixture. Cook 3 to 4 minutes, without stirring, until egg mixture begins to set around edge. Place skillet in oven and bake 10 to 12 minutes or until frittata is set and knife inserted in center comes out clean. Cut into wedges to serve.

EACH SERVING About 250 calories | 17 g protein | 6 g carbohydrate | 18 g total fat (6 g saturated) | 440 mg cholesterol | 680 mg sodium.

Spinach Strata

Whether you're serving it for brunch or dinner, you can assemble this a day ahead, then pop it in the oven—right from the refrigerator—just one hour before serving. All you need on the side is sliced tomatoes drizzled with vinaigrette dressing.

PREP 15 minutes plus refrigerating   BAKE 1 hour   MAKES 6 main-dish servings

8 slices firm white bread

4 ounces mozzarella cheese, shredded (1 cup)

1 package (10 ounces) frozen chopped spinach, thawed and squeezed dry

1 tablespoon butter or margarine, softened

2 cups milk

6 large eggs

½ cup loosely packed fresh basil leaves, chopped

½ teaspoon salt

¼ teaspoon coarsely ground black pepper

1. Grease 8" by 8" glass baking dish. Place 4 slices bread in dish; top with ½ cup cheese, all spinach, then remaining cheese. Spread butter on 1 side of remaining bread slices; place in dish, buttered side up.

2. In medium bowl, with wire whisk or fork, beat milk, eggs, basil, salt, and pepper until blended. Slowly pour mixture over bread slices. Prick bread with fork and press slices down to absorb egg mixture.

3. Cover baking dish with plastic wrap and refrigerate at least 30 minutes or overnight.

4. To bake, preheat oven to 350°F. Uncover baking dish and bake strata 1 hour or until knife inserted in center comes out clean. Remove the strata from the oven and let stand for 5 minutes.

EACH SERVING About 290 calories | 7 g protein | 22 g carbohydrate | 15 g total fat (6 g saturated) | 240 mg cholesterol | 575 mg sodium.

GH Test Kitchen Tip

If you like, add ½ cup finely chopped ham to the spinach layer when assembling the strata.

Mexican Potato Frittata

This flat, baked omelet combines a jar of salsa with a bit of sharp Cheddar cheese. While the frittata bakes, toss a package of prewashed baby spinach with sliced red onions, sliced fresh pears, and bottled salad dressing for a superquick salad to go with it.

PREP 5 minutes **COOK** 10 minutes **MAKES** 4 main-dish servings

1 teaspoon olive oil

12 ounces red-skinned potatoes, cut into ½-inch cubes

6 large eggs

1 jar (11 to 12 ounces) medium-hot salsa

½ teaspoon salt

¼ teaspoon coarsely ground black pepper

¼ cup shredded sharp Cheddar cheese (1 ounce)

1 medium tomato, diced

1. Preheat oven to 425°F. In nonstick 10-inch skillet with oven-safe handle (or cover handle with heavy-duty foil for baking in oven later), heat olive oil over medium-high heat; add potatoes and cook, covered, until potatoes are tender and golden brown, about 10 minutes, stirring occasionally.

2. Meanwhile, in medium bowl, with wire whisk or fork, beat eggs with ¼ cup salsa (chopped, if necessary), salt, and pepper. Stir in cheese; set aside. Stir diced tomato into remaining salsa.

3. Stir egg mixture into potatoes in skillet and cook over medium heat, covered, 3 minutes or until the egg mixture begins to set around edge. Remove cover and place skillet in oven; bake 4 to 6 minutes, until frittata is set.

4. To serve, invert frittata onto cutting board. Cut into wedges and top with salsa mixture.

EACH SERVING About 235 calories | 14 g protein | 20 g carbohydrate | 11 g total fat (4 g saturated) | 327 mg cholesterol | 795 mg sodium.

Eggplant Parmesan

We cut the fat in this Italian favorite with delicious results by oven-roasting the eggplant instead of breading and frying it. Then we topped it off with a cheesy, golden crust of mozzarella, Parmesan, and bread crumbs.

PREP 1 hour plus standing   BAKE about 1 hour   MAKES 6 main-dish servings

TOMATO SAUCE

1 tablespoon olive oil

1 medium onion, finely chopped

4 garlic cloves, minced

2 cans (28 ounces each) whole tomatoes in puree

1/4 cup tomato paste

1 teaspoon salt

1/4 teaspoon coarsely ground black pepper

1/4 cup loosely packed fresh basil leaves, chopped (optional)

EGGPLANT

3 medium eggplants (about 3 1/4 pounds), cut lengthwise into 1/2-inch-thick slices

2 tablespoons olive oil

1/2 teaspoon salt

BREAD-CRUMB TOPPING

2 teaspoons butter or margarine

2 slices firm white bread, coarsely grated

1 garlic clove, minced

2 ounces part-skim mozzarella cheese, shredded (1/2 cup)

2 tablespoons grated Parmesan cheese

CHEESE FILLING

1 container (15 ounces) part-skim ricotta cheese

2 ounces part-skim mozzarella cheese, shredded (1/2 cup)

2 tablespoons grated Parmesan cheese

1/4 teaspoon coarsely ground black pepper

1. Prepare Tomato Sauce: In 4-quart saucepan, heat oil over medium heat until hot. Add onion and cook until tender, about 8 minutes, stirring occasionally. Add garlic and cook 1 minute, stirring frequently.

2. Stir in tomatoes with their puree, tomato paste, salt, and pepper, breaking up tomatoes with side of spoon; heat to boiling over high heat. Reduce heat to low and simmer, uncovered, 25 minutes or until sauce thickens slightly. Stir in basil. Makes about 6 cups. (Cover and refrigerate 2 cups sauce for another use; see Tip.)

3. While sauce is simmering, prepare eggplant: Preheat oven to 450°F. Grease 2 large cookie sheets. Arrange the eggplant slices in single layer on cookie sheets. Brush top of eggplant slices with olive oil and sprinkle with salt.

4. Bake eggplant slices 25 to 30 minutes or until tender and golden, rotating sheets and turning slices over halfway through cooking. Remove eggplant from oven and turn oven control to 350°F.

5. Prepare Bread-Crumb Topping: In nonstick 10-inch skillet, melt butter over medium heat. Add grated bread and garlic, and cook about 7 minutes or until lightly browned, stirring occasionally. Transfer to small bowl. Add mozzarella and Parmesan; toss until evenly mixed.

6. Prepare Cheese Filling: In medium bowl, mix ricotta, mozzarella, Parmesan, and pepper until blended.

7. Assemble casserole: Into 13" by 9" glass baking dish, evenly spoon 1 cup tomato sauce. Arrange half of eggplant, overlapping slightly, in baking dish; top with 1 cup tomato sauce then dollops of cheese filling. Top cheese with 1 cup tomato sauce, remaining eggplant, and remaining tomato sauce (about 1 cup). Sprinkle casserole with the bread-crumb topping.

8. Cover dish with foil and bake casserole 15 minutes. Uncover and bake 15 minutes longer or until hot and bubbly. Let stand 10 minutes for easier serving.

EACH SERVING About 380 calories | 21 g protein | 35 g carbohydrate | 19 g total fat (8 g saturated) | 39 mg cholesterol | 1,385 mg sodium.

GH Test Kitchen Tip
Freeze the leftover sauce and use it over pasta or polenta.

Cabbage and Bulgur Casserole

We layered Napa cabbage with a filling that is healthy and tastes good too. Nutty-tasting bulgur is an especially easy grain to cook with because it doesn't need to be watched or stirred—you simply let it absorb boiling water until tender.

PREP 45 minutes   **BAKE** 40 minutes   **MAKES** 6 main-dish servings

1½ cups bulgur (cracked wheat)

1 tablespoon vegetable oil

2 medium carrots, peeled and diced

2 medium stalks celery, diced

1 medium red pepper, diced

½ small head Napa (Chinese) cabbage (about 1¾ pounds), cut crosswise into 2-inch pieces to equal about 12 cups leafy tops and 2 cups crunchy stems

3 garlic cloves, crushed with garlic press

3 green onions, sliced

2 tablespoons minced, peeled fresh ginger

2 tablespoons plus 1 teaspoon soy sauce

2 tablespoons seasoned rice vinegar

1 can (14½ ounces) diced tomatoes

2 tablespoons brown sugar

2 tablespoons chopped fresh parsley leaves for garnish

1. Preheat the oven to 350°F. In a 2-quart saucepan, heat *1½ cups water* to boiling over high heat; stir in bulgur. Remove saucepan from heat; cover and set aside.

2. In 5-quart Dutch oven, heat vegetable oil over medium-high heat. Add carrots, celery, and red pepper; cook 5 minutes. Add cabbage stems and cook 7 minutes longer or until vegetables are tender.

3. Reduce heat to low; add garlic, green onions, and ginger and cook 1 minute longer, stirring. Add *½ cup water*; heat to boiling over high heat. Reduce heat to low; simmer 1 minute, stirring. Remove Dutch oven from heat; stir in 2 tablespoons of the soy sauce, 1 tablespoon rice vinegar, and cooked bulgur.

4. In small bowl, combine the tomatoes with their juice, brown sugar, the remaining 1 tablespoon rice vinegar, and 1 teaspoon soy sauce.

5. In 3-quart casserole, place half of cabbage leaves; top with the bulgur mixture, then remaining cabbage leaves. Spoon tomato mixture over top. Cover casserole and bake 40 minutes or until hot in the center and top layer of cabbage leaves is wilted. Sprinkle with chopped parsley before serving.

EACH SERVING About 220 calories | 7 g protein | 43 g carbohydrate | 3 g total fat (0 g saturated) | 0 mg cholesterol | 800 mg sodium.

Stir-Fries & Skillet Suppers

**Butternut-Squash
Risotto with Sage**

Spicy Tangerine Beef

Sweet, juicy tangerines are the perfect complement to beef and broccoli. Sliced pork tenderloin can be substituted for the beef, if you prefer.

🍊 **PREP** 25 minutes   **COOK** 25 minutes   **MAKES** 4 main-dish servings

4 tangerines or 3 medium navel oranges

3 tablespoons vegetable oil

I boneless beef top sirloin steak (12 ounces), thinly sliced crosswise

2 tablespoons plus ½ teaspoon cornstarch

I large bunch broccoli (1½ pounds), cut into flowerets, stems peeled and cut into ¼-inch-thick slices

3 medium green onions, cut diagonally into 2-inch pieces

I medium red pepper, thinly sliced

3 garlic cloves, minced

I tablespoon minced, peeled fresh ginger

3 tablespoons soy sauce

¼ teaspoon crushed red pepper

1. Cut peel and white pith from 1 tangerine or orange. Over small bowl, cut on either side of membranes to remove each segment, allowing fruit and juice to drop into bowl; set aside. From remaining fruit, with vegetable peeler, remove eight 3-inch-long strips peel (about ¾ inch wide each). With knife, remove any pith from peel. Squeeze ¾ cup juice.

2. In 12-inch skillet, heat 2 tablespoons vegetable oil over high heat until hot. Add strips of peel and cook until lightly browned, about 3 minutes. Remove peel to large bowl.

3. Meanwhile, on waxed paper, toss beef slices with 2 tablespoons cornstarch to coat evenly. Cook half of beef until crisp and lightly browned on both sides, about 5 minutes; remove to bowl with peel. Repeat with remaining 1 tablespoon vegetable oil and beef.

4. Add broccoli and *2 tablespoons water* to skillet. Reduce heat to medium; cover and cook 2 minutes. Increase heat to high. Remove cover and add green onions and red pepper; cook 2 minutes, stirring. Add garlic and ginger; cook 1 minute longer.

5. Meanwhile, in cup, stir juice, soy sauce, crushed red pepper, and the remaining ½ teaspoon cornstarch until blended.

6. Add juice mixture and cook until sauce thickens slightly and boils, stirring. Return beef mixture to skillet. Add citrus segments with any juice in bowl; gently toss to combine.

EACH SERVING About 335 calories | 22 g protein | 24 g carbohydrate | 19 g total fat (4 g saturated) | 42 mg cholesterol | 860 mg sodium.

Beef Stir-Fry with Arugula

For a speedy weeknight meal, there's nothing like a stir-fry. To round out the menu, serve this one over rice or couscous with chilled red grapes for dessert.

PREP 10 minutes   **COOK** 10 minutes   **MAKES** 4 main-dish servings

4 teaspoons vegetable oil

1 bunch green onions, cut into 1½-inch pieces

1 package (8 ounces) sliced mushrooms

1 package (16 ounces) sliced beef for stir-fry (see **Tip**)

3 tablespoons soy sauce

3 tablespoons balsamic vinegar

2 tablespoons brown sugar

2 bunches arugula or 2 packages (8 ounces each) prewashed spinach

1. In nonstick 12-inch skillet, heat 2 teaspoons oil over medium-high heat. Add green onions and mushrooms and cook until tender and brown, about 5 minutes, stirring often. Remove to bowl.

2. In same skillet, heat 1 teaspoon oil. Add half the beef and cook, stirring constantly, until beef just loses its pink color. Remove to bowl with vegetables. Cook remaining beef as above, adding remaining 1 teaspoon oil.

3. In cup, mix soy sauce, balsamic vinegar, and brown sugar. Return beef mixture to skillet; stir in soy-sauce mixture. Cook 1 minute to heat through, stirring. Remove from heat; stir in half the arugula.

4. Spoon the beef mixture over remaining arugula on platter.

EACH SERVING About 260 calories | 29 g protein | 18 g carbohydrate | 15 g total fat (5 g saturated) | 48 mg cholesterol | 875 mg sodium.

GH Test Kitchen Tip

If you can't find precut beef, thinly slice a 1-pound piece of round steak.

Steak and Oven Fries

We used lean flank steak and cooked the "fries" in the oven to make this very delicious lower-fat version of steak frites.

PREP 15 minutes   COOK 20 to 25 minutes   MAKES 4 main-dish servings

Oven Fries (recipe follows)

I beef flank steak (1 pound)

¼ teaspoon coarsely ground black pepper

2 teaspoons olive oil

I large shallot, minced (about ¼ cup)

½ cup dry red wine

½ cup chicken broth

2 tablespoons chopped fresh parsley

1. Prepare Oven Fries.

2. Meanwhile, sprinkle steak on both sides with pepper. Heat nonstick 12-inch skillet over medium-high heat until hot. Add steak and cook about 14 minutes for medium-rare or until of desired doneness, turning once. Remove steak to cutting board; keep warm.

3. To drippings in skillet, add olive oil; heat over medium heat until hot. Add shallot and cook 2 minutes or until golden, stirring occasionally. Increase heat to medium-high. Add red wine and chicken broth; heat to boiling. Cook 3 to 4 minutes. Stir in parsley.

4. To serve, holding knife almost parallel to cutting surface, thinly slice steak. Spoon red-wine sauce over steak slices and serve with Oven Fries.

OVEN FRIES Preheat oven to 500°F. Spray two 15½" by 10½" jelly-roll pans or 2 large cookie sheets with nonstick cooking spray. Scrub 4 medium unpeeled baking potatoes (2 pounds) well but do not peel. Cut each potato lengthwise in half. Holding each potato half flat side down, cut lengthwise into ¼-inch-thick slices, then cut each slice lengthwise into ¼-inch-wide sticks. Place potatoes in medium bowl and toss with ½ teaspoon salt and ¼ teaspoon black pepper. Divide potato sticks equally between pans. Place pans on 2 oven racks and bake potatoes 20 to 25 minutes, until tender and lightly browned, turning potatoes once with pancake turner and rotating pans between upper and lower racks halfway through the baking time.

EACH SERVING About 390 calories | 31 g protein | 40 g carbohydrate | 11 g total fat (4 g saturated) | 46 mg cholesterol | 455 mg sodium.

Corned Beef with Cabbage and Potatoes

A horseradish-mustard sauce dresses up an old favorite. Prepare the recipe over the weekend, then use the leftovers to make Red Flannel Hash (page 74) during the week, when time is at a premium.

PREP 30 minutes   **COOK** 3 hours 25 minutes   **MAKES** 8 main-dish servings

CORNED BEEF AND VEGETABLES

1 corned-beef brisket (about 4½ pounds), trimmed of excess fat

20 whole black peppercorns

5 whole allspice

5 garlic cloves, unpeeled

2 bay leaves

4 pounds all-purpose potatoes, peeled and each cut into quarters

1 pound carrots, peeled

1 pound parsnips, peeled

1 medium head green cabbage (about 3 pounds), cut into 8 wedges, with core attached

HORSERADISH-MUSTARD SAUCE

½ cup **Dijon mustard with seeds**

2 tablespoons pure maple syrup

1 tablespoon prepared white horseradish

chopped parsley for garnish

1. Prepare Corned Beef and Vegetables: In 8-quart Dutch oven or saucepot, place brisket, peppercorns, allspice, garlic, bay leaves, and enough *water* to cover; heat to boiling over high heat. Reduce heat to low; cover and simmer 2 hours 30 minutes.

2. Add quartered potatoes, whole carrots, and whole parsnips to Dutch oven; heat to boiling over high heat. Reduce heat to low; cover and simmer 30 minutes or until meat and vegetables are tender. With tongs and slotted spoon, transfer meat and vegetables to platter; cover and keep warm.

3. Add cabbage to liquid in Dutch oven; heat to boiling over high heat. Reduce heat to low; cover and simmer 5 minutes or until cabbage is tender.

4. Meanwhile, prepare Horseradish-Mustard Sauce: In small bowl, with fork, mix mustard, maple syrup, and horseradish until smooth; set sauce aside.

5. Drain cabbage and add to platter with meat. Thinly slice meat and serve with vegetables and Horseradish-Mustard Sauce. Garnish with chopped parsley.

EACH SERVING About 520 calories | 41 g protein | 64 g carbohydrate | 12 g total fat (4 g saturated) | 105 mg cholesterol | 1,450 mg sodium.

Red Flannel Hash

The trick to great hash is to avoid overstirring. Let it cook undisturbed long enough to become crisp and golden. Serve by the plateful with a cucumber-and-dill salad.

PREP 15 minutes   **COOK** 30 minutes   **MAKES** 4 main-dish servings

1 tablespoon butter or margarine

1 tablespoon vegetable oil

1 jumbo onion (about 1 pound), chopped

2 large stalks celery, cut into ½-inch pieces

1 can (14½ ounces) whole beets, drained and cut into ½-inch pieces

4 cups bite-size pieces cooked potatoes (reserved from Corned Beef with Cabbage and Potatoes, page 72)

1½ cups bite-size pieces cooked corned beef (reserved from Corned Beef with Cabbage and Potatoes, page 72), about 6 ounces

½ teaspoon salt

¼ teaspoon coarsely ground black pepper

1 tablespoon chopped fresh parsley leaves

1. In nonstick 12-inch skillet, heat butter with oil over medium heat. Add onion and celery and cook 15 minutes or until lightly browned and tender, stirring occasionally.

2. Increase heat to medium-high; add beets, potatoes, corned beef, salt, and pepper, and cook 15 minutes or until browned, stirring occasionally. Sprinkle with parsley to serve.

EACH SERVING About 415 calories | 19 g protein | 62 g carbohydrate | 11 g total fat (3 g saturated) | 40 mg cholesterol | 1,065 mg sodium.

Spicy Peanut Pork

Asian spices and peanut butter turn pork chops into a sensational supper. Try this tasty combination over steamed rice or Asian noodles.

PREP 15 minutes   COOK about 15 minutes   MAKES 4 main-dish servings

4 boneless pork loin chops, ¾ inch thick (5 ounces each), well trimmed

¼ teaspoon coarsely ground black pepper

½ teaspoon salt

4 medium green onions, cut into 1-inch diagonal slices

8 ounces snow peas, strings removed

1 tablespoon minced, peeled fresh ginger

3 garlic cloves, crushed with garlic press

¼ cup creamy peanut butter

1 tablespoon sugar

1 tablespoon soy sauce

⅛ teaspoon ground red pepper (cayenne)

¾ cup water

1. Pat pork chops dry with paper towels. Sprinkle pork chops with pepper and ¼ teaspoon salt.

2. Heat nonstick 12-inch skillet over medium-high heat until hot. Add pork chops and cook 4 minutes; turn pork over and cook 3 to 4 minutes longer, until lightly browned on the outside and still slightly pink on the inside. Transfer pork to platter; cover with foil to keep warm.

3. To same skillet, add green onions, snow peas, and remaining ¼ teaspoon salt, and cook over medium heat 4 minutes, stirring frequently. Stir in ginger and garlic; cook 1 minute. Return pork to skillet.

4. Meanwhile, in small bowl, stir peanut butter, sugar, soy sauce, ground red pepper, and water until blended.

5. Pour peanut-butter mixture into same skillet; heat to boiling over medium-high heat. Reduce heat to low; simmer 1 minute.

EACH SERVING About 350 calories | 37 g protein | 13 g carbohydrate | 17 g total fat (5 g saturated) | 76 mg cholesterol | 685 mg sodium.

Orange Pork and Asparagus Stir-Fry

Asparagus is graded by size: small, standard, large, and jumbo. All are equally tender, but we call for thin asparagus here because it cooks quickly.

PREP 20 minutes   COOK about 6 minutes   MAKES 4 main-dish servings

2 navel oranges

1 teaspoon olive oil

1 whole pork tenderloin (about 12 ounces) trimmed, thinly sliced diagonally

¾ teaspoon salt

¼ teaspoon ground black pepper

1½ pounds thin asparagus, trimmed and each stalk cut in half

1 garlic clove, crushed with garlic press

¼ cup water

kumquats on the stem for garnish (optional)

1. From 1 orange, grate 1 teaspoon peel and squeeze ¼ cup juice. Cut off peel and white pith from remaining orange. Cut orange into ¼-inch slices; cut each slice into quarters.

2. In nonstick 12-inch skillet, heat ½ teaspoon oil over medium-high heat until hot but not smoking. Add half the pork and sprinkle with ¼ teaspoon salt and ⅛ teaspoon pepper; cook 2 minutes or until pork just loses its pink color, stirring frequently. Transfer pork to plate. Repeat with remaining ½ teaspoon oil, pork, ¼ teaspoon salt, and remaining ⅛ teaspoon pepper. Transfer pork to same plate.

3. To same skillet, add asparagus, garlic, orange peel, remaining ¼ teaspoon salt, and water; cover and cook about 2 minutes or until asparagus is tender crisp, stirring occasionally. Return pork to skillet. Add orange juice and orange pieces; heat through, stirring often. Garnish with kumquats if you like.

EACH SERVING About 165 calories | 24 g protein | 8 g carbohydrate | 4 g total fat (1 g saturated) | 50 mg cholesterol | 495 mg sodium.

Polenta with Sausage and Peppers

We used ready-to-slice polenta from the refrigerated section of the supermarket, making this dish super-easy to prepare.

⏲ **PREP** 15 minutes   **COOK** 25 minutes   **MAKES** 4 main-dish servings

12 ounces hot and/or sweet Italian-sausage links, casings removed

1 package (24 ounces) precooked polenta, cut into 16 slices

1 tablespoon olive oil

1 medium onion, thinly sliced

1 medium red pepper, thinly sliced

1 garlic clove, crushed with garlic press

½ cup chicken broth

1. Preheat broiler. Heat nonstick 12-inch skillet over medium-high heat until hot. Add sausage and cook until browned, about 10 minutes, stirring occasionally and breaking up sausage with side of spoon. With slotted spoon, transfer sausage to medium bowl; wipe skillet clean with paper towels.

2. Spray 15½" by 10½" jelly-roll pan with nonstick cooking spray. Place polenta slices in pan; spray to coat. With pan at closest position to source of heat, broil polenta slices 10 minutes, turning slices over halfway through cooking.

3. Meanwhile, in same skillet, heat olive oil over medium-high heat until hot. Add onion and pepper and cook until tender and lightly browned, 8 to 10 minutes, stirring occasionally. Add garlic and sausage; cook 1 minute, stirring. Add chicken broth and heat to boiling. Return mixture to bowl; keep warm.

4. Serve the polenta slices topped with the sausage mixture.

EACH SERVING About 360 calories | 12 g protein | 31 g carbohydrate | 21 g total fat (6 g saturated) | 45 mg cholesterol | 1,150 mg sodium.

Kielbasa and Red Cabbage

It's worth a trip to a Polish butcher for homemade kielbasa to make this stick-to-your-ribs skillet meal.

PREP 15 minutes   COOK 40 minutes   MAKES 4 main-dish servings

2 tablespoons butter or margarine

1 small onion, chopped

1 small head red cabbage (1½ pounds), thinly sliced

2 Golden Delicious apples, peeled, cored, and thinly sliced

½ cup apple juice

3 tablespoons red wine vinegar

1 tablespoon sugar

1 teaspoon salt

1 pound kielbasa (smoked Polish sausage), cut crosswise into 2-inch pieces

1. In nonstick 10-inch skillet, melt butter over medium heat. Add onion and cook, stirring, until tender. Add cabbage, apples, apple juice, vinegar, sugar, and salt; heat to boiling. Reduce heat to low; cover and simmer for 15 minutes.

2. Add kielbasa to cabbage mixture; heat to boiling over high heat. Reduce heat; cover and simmer 15 minutes.

EACH SERVING About 524 calories | 18 g protein | 32 g carbohydrate | 37 g total fat (15 g saturated) | 92 mg cholesterol | 1,883 mg sodium.

GH Test Kitchen Tip

We used Golden Delicious for this dish, but Gala, Fuji, or Jonagold would also be good.

Cutlets Romano with Arugula Salad

A flavor-packed coating of bread crumbs and grated cheese adds terrific taste to chicken breasts. We serve them over an arugula and red pepper salad to make an Italian-style meal-in-one.

PREP 25 minutes   **COOK** about 8 minutes   **MAKES** 4 main-dish servings

ARUGULA SALAD

2 tablespoons fresh lemon juice

1 tablespoon olive oil

½ teaspoon sugar

⅛ teaspoon salt

⅛ teaspoon coarsely ground black pepper

1 jar (7 ounces) roasted red peppers, drained and thinly sliced

2 bags (3 to 4 ounces each) arugula or 1 bag (about 6 ounces) baby spinach

CHICKEN CUTLETS

½ cup plain dried bread crumbs

⅓ cup grated Romano cheese

¼ teaspoon salt

¼ teaspoon coarsely ground black pepper

1 large egg

4 small skinless, boneless chicken-breast halves (about 1 pound), pounded to ¼-inch thickness

1 tablespoon olive oil

lemon wedges

1. Prepare Arugula Salad: In large bowl, with wire whisk or fork, mix lemon juice, olive oil, sugar, salt, and black pepper. Add red peppers and toss to coat; place arugula on top and set salad aside.

2. Prepare Chicken Cutlets: On waxed paper, combine bread crumbs, Romano cheese, salt, and pepper. In pie plate, beat egg with fork. Dip chicken cutlets into egg, then into crumb mixture to coat both sides.

3. In nonstick 12-inch skillet, heat 1½ teaspoons oil over medium-high heat until hot. Add half of cutlets and cook about 2 minutes per side or just until chicken loses its pink color inside and is golden brown outside. Repeat with remaining oil and cutlets.

4. To serve, toss Arugula Salad and spoon onto 4 dinner plates. Arrange cutlets on top of salad. Serve with lemon wedges.

EACH SERVING About 320 calories | 34 g protein | 17 g carbohydrate | 13 g total fat (3 g saturated) | 128 mg cholesterol | 665 mg sodium.

Spaghetti Squash with Smoked Mozzarella and Chicken

We microwaved the squash to speed up the cooking time. While it cooks, sauté the onion and chicken.

🕐 PREP 15 minutes   MICROWAVE 12 to 14 minutes   MAKES 4 main-dish servings

1 medium spaghetti squash (about 2½ pounds)

1 tablespoon olive oil

1 large onion, thinly sliced

12 ounces chicken breast cut for stir-fry

½ teaspoon salt

¼ teaspoon coarsely ground black pepper

2 medium tomatoes, diced

2 ounces smoked mozzarella or smoked Gouda cheese

¼ cup loosely packed fresh basil leaves, thinly sliced

1. With tip of sharp knife, pierce squash in about 10 places. Microwave on High 6 to 7 minutes. Turn squash over and pierce in another 10 places; microwave 6 to 7 minutes longer or until squash is soft to the touch.

2. Meanwhile, in nonstick 12-inch skillet, heat olive oil over medium heat. Add onion and cook until tender and golden, about 8 minutes, stirring occasionally.

3. Add chicken, ¼ teaspoon salt, and ⅛ teaspoon pepper and cook until chicken loses its pink color throughout, about 8 minutes, stirring occasionally.

4. When squash is done, cut lengthwise in half; discard seeds. With fork, gently scrape squash lengthwise and lift out pulp in strands as it becomes free; place in large bowl. Discard squash skin.

5. Mix tomatoes, cheese, and remaining ¼ teaspoon salt and ⅛ teaspoon pepper with hot squash. Spoon squash mixture into 4 serving bowls; top with onion and chicken mixture. Sprinkle with basil.

EACH SERVING About 260 calories | 25 g protein | 20 g carbohydrate | 9 g total fat (3 g saturated) | 62 mg cholesterol | 585 mg sodium.

Skillet Arroz con Pollo

This dish, popular in Spain and Mexico, literally means "rice with chicken." We've used chicken-breast tenders instead of bone-in pieces to shorten cooking time.

PREP 15 minutes **COOK** about 40 minutes **MAKES** 4 main-dish servings

1 tablespoon olive oil

1 medium onion, finely chopped

1 medium red pepper, cut into 1½-inch pieces

1 cup long-grain white rice

1 garlic clove, minced

⅛ teaspoon ground red pepper (cayenne)

1 strip (3" by ½") fresh lemon peel

¼ teaspoon salt

1 can (14½ ounces) chicken broth

¼ cup dry sherry or water

1 pound chicken-breast tenders, cut into 2-inch pieces

1 cup frozen peas

¼ cup drained salad olives (chopped pimiento-stuffed olives)

½ cup loosely packed fresh cilantro leaves or parsley leaves, chopped

lemon wedges

1. In nonstick 12-inch skillet, heat oil over medium heat until hot. Add onion and red pepper and cook until tender, about 12 minutes, stirring occasionally. Stir in rice, garlic, and ground red pepper; cook 2 minutes. Stir in lemon peel, salt, chicken broth, and sherry; heat to boiling over medium-high heat. Reduce heat to low; cover and simmer for 13 minutes.

2. Stir in chicken tenders; cover and simmer 13 minutes longer or until juices run clear when chicken is pierced with tip of knife and rice is tender, stirring once halfway through cooking time. Stir in frozen peas; cover and heat through. Remove skillet from heat; let stand 5 minutes.

3. To serve, stir in olives and sprinkle with cilantro. Pass lemon wedges to squeeze over each serving.

EACH SERVING About 410 calories | 34 g protein | 49 g carbohydrate | 7 g total fat (2 g saturated) | 66 mg cholesterol | 925 mg sodium.

Thai Chicken with Asparagus

A trio of Asian seasonings—ginger, chiles, and Asian fish sauce—turns up the heat in this skillet dinner. If you prefer, use fresh green beans instead of the asparagus.

PREP 25 minutes   COOK 30 minutes   MAKES 4 main-dish servings

I teaspoon salt

I pound thin asparagus, trimmed and cut diagonally into 3-inch pieces

I tablespoon sugar

3 tablespoons Asian fish sauce (see Tip)

2 tablespoons fresh lime juice

I tablespoon plus I teaspoon soy sauce

4 medium skinless, boneless chicken-breast halves (about 1¼ pounds), thinly sliced

3 teaspoons vegetable oil

I jumbo onion (about I pound), thinly sliced

I piece fresh ginger (about 2" by 1"), peeled and cut into matchstick-thin strips

2 jalapeño chiles, seeded and cut into matchstick-thin strips

2 cups packed fresh basil leaves

I cup packed fresh cilantro leaves

I. In 10-inch skillet, heat *1 inch water* and salt to boiling over high heat. Add asparagus; heat to boiling. Reduce heat to low; simmer, uncovered, 3 to 5 minutes, until asparagus is just tender-crisp. Drain asparagus; set aside.

2. In medium bowl, mix sugar, fish sauce, lime juice, and soy sauce. Stir in chicken until evenly coated. (Coat chicken just before cooking, because the lime juice will change its texture.)

3. In nonstick 12-inch skillet, heat 2 teaspoons oil over medium-high heat until hot. Add chicken and cook 5 minutes or just until it loses its pink color throughout, stirring occasionally. With tongs or slotted spoon, transfer chicken to a clean bowl, leaving any cooking liquid in skillet.

4. Add onion, ginger, and jalapeños to skillet and cook until onion is tender, about 8 minutes. Transfer onion mixture to bowl with the cooked chicken.

5. In same skillet, heat remaining 1 teaspoon oil over medium heat until hot. Add the asparagus to the skillet and cook until it begins to brown, about 5 minutes, stirring occasionally. Return onion mixture and chicken to skillet; heat through.

6. Toss basil and cilantro leaves with chicken mixture just before serving.

EACH SERVING About 290 calories | 38 g protein | 21 g carbohydrate | 6 g total fat (1 g saturated) | 82 mg cholesterol | 1,555 mg sodium.

GH Test Kitchen Tip

Asian fish sauce (nuoc nam or nam pla) is available in specialty sections of some supermarkets or in Asian groceries.

Chicken Breasts with Vegetable Ribbons

Lemon peel, garlic, and parsley add easy elegance and bursts of flavor. An ordinary vegetable peeler is all you need to make the vegetable ribbons.

PREP 15 minutes **COOK** 25 minutes **MAKES** 4 main-dish servings

4 medium skinless, boneless chicken-breast halves (about 1¼ pounds)

¼ teaspoon coarsely ground black pepper

½ teaspoon salt

2 garlic cloves, minced

2 teaspoons freshly grated lemon peel

1 tablespoon olive oil

3 medium carrots, peeled

2 medium zucchini (about 8 ounces each)

¾ cup chicken broth

1 cup loosely packed fresh parsley leaves, chopped

1. Sprinkle chicken with pepper and ¼ teaspoon salt. In cup, mix garlic, lemon peel, and remaining ¼ teaspoon salt; set aside.

2. In 12-inch skillet, heat oil over medium-high heat until hot. Add chicken and cook 6 minutes. Reduce heat to medium; turn chicken over and cook 6 to 8 minutes longer, until juices run clear when thickest part of breast is pierced with tip of knife.

3. Meanwhile, with sharp vegetable peeler, peel carrots lengthwise into wide, thin strips. Repeat with zucchini.

4. Transfer chicken to plate; sprinkle with garlic mixture and keep warm. In same skillet, heat broth and *¼ cup water* to boiling over high heat. Reduce heat to medium-low; add carrots and cook, covered, 3 minutes. Add zucchini and cook, covered, 5 to 7 minutes longer, until vegetables are just tender. Stir in all but 1 tablespoon parsley.

5. To serve, spoon vegetable ribbons and broth onto 4 dinner plates; top with chicken. Sprinkle with remaining parsley.

EACH SERVING About 240 calories | 36 g protein | 0 g carbohydrate | 6 g total fat (1 g saturated) | 82 mg cholesterol | 530 mg sodium.

Peachy Chicken with Basil

Fragrant basil, sweet onion, and juicy fruit slices form the perfect sauce for lean chicken breasts. Spoon over noodles or rice to capture every luscious drop.

PREP 20 minutes   COOK 15 minutes   MAKES 4 main-dish servings

3 tablespoons all-purpose flour

½ teaspoon salt

½ teaspoon coarsely ground black pepper

4 medium skinless, boneless chicken-breast halves (about 1¼ pounds)

2 tablespoons butter or margarine

¾ cup chicken broth

3 medium peaches (about 1 pound), peeled and sliced

1 small red onion, thinly sliced

¼ teaspoon freshly grated lemon peel

8 large basil leaves, thinly sliced

1. On waxed paper, mix flour, salt, and pepper. Coat the chicken breasts with the seasoned flour.

2. In nonstick 12-inch skillet, melt butter over medium heat. Add chicken and cook 10 to 12 minutes, until juices run clear when thickest part of chicken breast is pierced with tip of knife, turning once. Transfer chicken to platter; keep warm.

3. Add chicken broth to skillet; heat to boiling over high heat. Add peaches, red onion, and lemon peel. Cook, stirring frequently, about 3 minutes or until peaches are softened and sauce is slightly thickened. Stir sliced basil into skillet.

4. Spoon sauce over chicken to serve.

EACH SERVING About 280 calories | 35 g protein | 16 g carbohydrate | 8 g total fat (2 g saturated) | 82 mg cholesterol | 580 mg sodium.

Shrimp Risotto with Baby Peas

Be sure to buy shrimp in the shells for this dish. Making a quick stock with the shells gives this pretty risotto a more complex flavor.

PREP 35 minutes   COOK 55 minutes   MAKES 4 main-dish servings

4 cups water

I can (14½ ounces) chicken or vegetable broth or 1¾ cups Chicken Broth (page 9) or Vegetable Broth (page 9)

I pound medium shrimp, shelled and deveined (page 11), shells reserved

I tablespoon butter or margarine

I½ teaspoons salt

⅛ teaspoon ground black pepper

I tablespoon olive oil

I small onion, finely chopped

2 cups Arborio rice (Italian short-grain rice) or medium-grain rice

½ cup dry white wine

I cup frozen baby peas

¼ cup chopped fresh parsley

1. In 3-quart saucepan, combine water, broth, and shrimp shells. Heat to boiling over high heat. Reduce heat; simmer 20 minutes. Strain broth through sieve into bowl and measure. If needed, add *water* to equal 5½ cups. Return broth to same clean saucepan; heat to boiling. Reduce heat to maintain simmer; cover.

2. In 4-quart saucepan, melt butter over medium-high heat. Add shrimp, ½ teaspoon salt, and pepper; cook, stirring, just until the shrimp are opaque throughout, about 2 minutes. Transfer to bowl.

3. In same saucepan, heat oil over medium heat. Add onion and cook until tender, about 5 minutes. Add rice and remaining 1 teaspoon salt; cook, stirring frequently, until rice grains are opaque. Add wine; cook until wine has been absorbed. Add about ½ cup simmering broth to rice; stir until liquid has been absorbed. Continue cooking, adding remaining broth ½ cup at a time and stirring after each addition, until all liquid has been absorbed and rice is tender but still firm, about 25 minutes (Risotto should have a creamy consistency.) Stir in frozen peas and shrimp and heat through. Stir in parsley.

EACH SERVING About 511 calories | 28 g protein | 76 g carbohydrate | 10 g total fat (3 g saturated) | 148 mg cholesterol | 1,532 mg sodium.

Shrimp Curry and Rice

This tastes as good as classic slow-cooked curry but is ready in a flash. Serve with crisp flatbreads such as pappadams.

PREP 10 minutes   **COOK** about 20 minutes   **MAKES** 4 main-dish servings

1 cup regular long-grain rice

2 teaspoons olive oil

1 medium onion, diced

1 tablespoon curry powder

1 teaspoon mustard seeds

1 pound shelled and deveined fresh or frozen (thawed) large shrimp with tail part of shell left on if you like

½ cup light coconut milk (not cream of coconut)

¾ cup frozen peas, thawed

1 cup frozen whole baby carrots, thawed

½ teaspoon salt

chopped fresh cilantro leaves (optional)

1. Prepare rice as label directs but do not add margarine or butter.

2. Meanwhile, in nonstick 12-inch skillet, heat 1 teaspoon olive oil over medium-high heat until hot. Reduce heat to medium; add onion and cook 8 minutes or until tender. Add curry powder and cook 1 minute, stirring. Transfer onion mixture to medium bowl.

3. Increase heat to medium-high. In same skillet, heat remaining 1 teaspoon olive oil until hot. Add mustard seeds; cook 30 seconds, stirring. Add the shrimp and cook 4 minutes or until opaque throughout, stirring frequently.

4. Return onion mixture to skillet; stir in coconut milk, peas, carrots, and salt; heat through. Serve over rice. Sprinkle with cilantro if you like.

EACH SERVING About 390 calories | 30 g protein | 49 g carbohydrate | 8 g total fat (2 g saturated) | 175 mg cholesterol | 490 mg sodium.

Chili Scallops with Black-Bean Salsa

A light dusting of spices makes tender sea scallops taste really special. The flavorful salsa can also be served as a side dish with grilled beef or chicken.

PREP 15 minutes   **COOK** 3 to 6 minutes   **MAKES** 4 main-dish servings

I can (15 to 19 ounces) black beans, rinsed and drained

I can (15¼ to 16 ounces) whole-kernel corn, drained

¼ cup finely chopped red onion

¼ cup loosely packed fresh cilantro leaves, chopped

2 tablespoons fresh lime juice

½ teaspoon salt

I pound sea scallops

I tablespoon chili powder

I teaspoon sugar

2 teaspoons vegetable oil

cilantro leaves and hot red chiles for garnish

lime wedges (optional)

1. In large bowl, mix black beans, corn, onion, chopped cilantro, lime juice, and ¼ teaspoon salt. Set black-bean salsa aside.

2. Rinse scallops with cold running water to remove sand from crevices; pat dry with paper towels. In medium bowl, mix chili powder, sugar, and remaining ¼ teaspoon salt; add scallops, tossing to coat.

3. In nonstick 12-inch skillet, heat vegetable oil over medium-high heat until very hot. Add scallops and cook 3 to 6 minutes until scallops are lightly browned on the outside and turn opaque throughout, turning once.

4. Arrange black-bean salsa and scallops on 4 dinner plates and garnish with cilantro leaves and red chiles. Serve with lime wedges if you like.

EACH SERVING About 290 calories | 31 g protein | 40 g carbohydrate | 5 g total fat (1 g saturated) | 38 mg cholesterol | 1,005 mg sodium.

Huevos Rancheros

This hearty Mexican dish is often served for brunch, but it makes a wonderful supper, too. Any of the following make great toppings: sliced avocado, black beans, mixed salad greens, and sour cream.

PREP 10 minutes **COOK** 20 minutes **MAKES** 4 main-dish servings

1 tablespoon plus 2 teaspoons vegetable oil

1 medium onion, coarsely chopped

1 small garlic clove, minced

1 jalapeño chile, seeded and minced

1 can (14½ ounces) tomatoes

¼ teaspoon salt

8 large eggs

8 flour or corn tortillas (6-inch diameter), warmed

1 tablespoon chopped fresh cilantro leaves

1. In 2-quart saucepan, heat 1 tablespoon vegetable oil over medium-high heat until hot. Add onion, garlic, and jalapeño, and cook until onion is tender, stirring occasionally, about 8 minutes. Stir in tomatoes with their juice and salt; heat to boiling over high heat, breaking up tomatoes with side of spoon. Reduce heat to low; cover and simmer 5 minutes, stirring occasionally.

2. In nonstick 10-inch skillet, heat 1 teaspoon vegetable oil over medium heat. One at a time, break 4 eggs into a saucer, then slip into skillet. Reduce heat to low; cook eggs slowly until whites are completely set and yolks begin to thicken but are not hard; turn eggs over if you like. Transfer eggs to warm plate; keep warm. Repeat with remaining 1 teaspoon oil and eggs.

3. Arrange tortillas on 4 dinner plates. Place 1 fried egg on each tortilla. Spoon 2 tablespoons tomato sauce over each egg; sprinkle with cilantro. Serve with remaining tomato sauce on the side.

EACH SERVING About 395 calories | 18 g protein | 37 g carbohydrate | 20 g total fat (4 g saturated) | 426 mg cholesterol | 665 mg sodium.

Fast Fried Rice

The secrets to this dish are quick-cooking brown rice, precut frozen vegetables, and ready-to-use stir-fry sauce.

⌚ **PREP** 5 minutes   **COOK** 10 minutes   **MAKES** 4 main-dish servings

1½ cups quick-cooking brown rice

1 pound firm tofu, drained and cut into
    1-inch cubes

6 teaspoons olive oil

1 package (16 ounces) frozen vegetables
    for stir-fry

2 large eggs, lightly beaten

⅓ cup stir-fry sauce

1. Prepare rice as label directs.

2. Meanwhile, in medium bowl, place 3 layers paper towels. Place tofu on towels and top with 3 more layers paper towels. Gently press the tofu with your hand to extract the excess moisture.

3. In nonstick 12-inch skillet, heat 2 teaspoons oil over medium-high heat until hot. Add frozen vegetables; cover and cook 5 minutes, stirring occasionally. Transfer vegetables to bowl; keep warm.

4. In same skillet, heat remaining 4 teaspoons oil until hot. Add tofu and cook 5 minutes, gently stirring. Stir in rice and cook 4 minutes longer.

5. With spatula, push rice mixture around edge of skillet, leaving space in center. Add eggs to center of skillet; cook 1 minute, stirring eggs until scrambled. Add stir-fry sauce, vegetables, and ¼ *cup water*; cook 1 minute, stirring.

EACH SERVING About 360 calories | 17 g protein | 41 g carbohydrate | 15 g total fat (2 g saturated) | 106 mg cholesterol | 760 mg sodium.

Butternut-Squash Risotto with Sage

This requires a lot of attention at the range, but it's worth it. If you can, use Arborio rice—it makes the dish extra creamy.

PREP 20 minutes   **COOK** 50 minutes   **MAKES** 4 main-dish servings

1 large butternut squash (2½ pounds), peeled

1 can (13¾ to 14½ ounces) chicken or vegetable broth

1 tablespoon butter or margarine

¼ teaspoon coarsely ground black pepper

3 tablespoons chopped fresh sage leaves

1 teaspoon salt

2 tablespoons olive oil

1 small onion, finely chopped

2 cups Arborio rice (Italian short-grain rice) or medium-grain rice

⅓ cup dry white wine

½ cup grated Parmesan cheese

1. Cut enough squash into ½-inch chunks to equal 3 cups. Coarsely shred enough remaining squash to equal 2 cups; set aside.

2. In 2-quart saucepan, heat broth and *4 cups water* to boiling over high heat. Reduce heat to low to maintain simmer; cover.

3. In 5-quart Dutch oven or saucepot, melt butter over medium heat. Add squash chunks, pepper, 2 tablespoons chopped sage, and ¼ teaspoon salt. Cook, covered, stirring occasionally, 10 minutes or until squash is tender. Remove squash to small bowl.

4. To same Dutch oven, add oil, shredded squash, onion, and remaining ¾ teaspoon salt and cook, stirring often, until vegetables are tender. Add rice and cook, stirring frequently, 2 minutes. Add wine; cook until absorbed. Add about ½ cup simmering broth to rice, stirring until liquid is absorbed.

5. Continue cooking, adding remaining broth, ½ cup at time, and stirring after each addition until all liquid is absorbed and rice is tender but still firm, about 25 minutes (risotto should have a creamy consistency). Stir in squash chunks, Parmesan, and remaining 1 tablespoon chopped sage and heat through.

EACH SERVING About 700 calories | 17 g protein | 115 g carbohydrate | 4 g total fat (4 g saturated) | 15 mg cholesterol | 1,105 mg sodium.

Pastas & Pies

**Caramelized Onion and
Goat Cheese Tart**

Beef and Sausage Lasagna

Always let lasagna stand for a good fifteen minutes after baking so the ingredients have time to settle—it makes for easier cutting.

🕐 **PREP** I hour **BAKE** 45 minutes **MAKES** 10 main-dish servings

8 ounces hot Italian-sausage links, casings removed

8 ounces ground beef chuck

1 medium onion, chopped

1 can (28 ounces) plum tomatoes

2 tablespoons tomato paste

1¼ teaspoons salt

12 lasagna noodles (10 ounces)

1 container (15 ounces) part-skim ricotta cheese

1 large egg

¼ cup chopped fresh parsley

⅛ teaspoon coarsely ground black pepper

8 ounces part-skim mozzarella cheese, shredded (2 cups)

1. Prepare meat sauce: In 4-quart saucepan, cook sausage, ground beef, and onion over high heat, breaking up sausage and meat with side of spoon, until meat is well browned. Discard fat. Add tomatoes with their juice, tomato paste, and 1 teaspoon salt. Heat to boiling, breaking up tomatoes with side of spoon. Reduce heat; cover and simmer, stirring occasionally, 30 minutes.

2. Meanwhile, in large saucepot, cook lasagna noodles as label directs but do not add salt to water. Drain and rinse with cold running water. Return to saucepot with *enough cold water to cover.*

3. Preheat oven to 375°F. In medium bowl, stir ricotta, egg, parsley, remaining ¼ teaspoon salt, and pepper until well combined.

4. Drain noodles on clean kitchen towels. In 13" by 9" baking dish, arrange 6 lasagna noodles, overlapping to fit. Spread with all of ricotta mixture and sprinkle with half of mozzarella; top with half of meat sauce. Cover with remaining 6 noodles and spread with remaining meat sauce. Sprinkle with remaining mozzarella.

5. Cover lasagna with foil and bake 30 minutes. Remove foil and bake until sauce is bubbling and top has lightly browned, about 15 minutes longer. Let stand 15 minutes for easier serving.

EACH SERVING About 363 calories | 23 g protein | 31 g carbohydrate | 16 g total fat (7 g saturated) | 74 mg cholesterol | 780 mg sodium.

Tamale Pie

Enjoy the great taste of tamales with less work. A green salad with grapefruit sections and sliced avocado makes a nice accompaniment.

⌀ PREP 25 minutes   BAKE 45 minutes   MAKES 6 main-dish servings

2 teaspoons vegetable oil

I medium onion, chopped

I pound ground beef chuck

I tablespoon chili powder

I teaspoon ground cumin

I cup medium-hot salsa

I can (15¼ to 16 ounces) whole-kernel
    corn, drained

4 cups water

I cup cornmeal

I teaspoon salt

2 ounces Cheddar cheese, shredded (½ cup)

I. Preheat oven to 350°F. In nonstick 12-inch skillet, heat oil over medium-high heat; add onion and cook until tender and golden, about 5 minutes. Stir in ground beef and cook, breaking up meat with side of spoon, until meat is browned, about 5 minutes. Skim and discard any fat. Stir in chili powder and cumin and cook 2 minutes longer. Remove from heat and stir in salsa and corn.

2. In 2-quart saucepan, heat water to boiling. With wire whisk, gradually whisk in cornmeal and salt. Cook over medium heat, whisking frequently, 5 minutes.

3. Pour half of cornmeal mixture into shallow 2-quart casserole. Spoon beef mixture over cornmeal; spoon remaining cornmeal over beef and sprinkle Cheddar on top. Bake 45 minutes. Remove casserole from oven and let stand 15 to 25 minutes before serving.

EACH SERVING About 334 calories | 21 g protein | 33 g carbohydrate | 13 g total fat (5 g saturated) | 57 mg cholesterol | 1,026 mg sodium.

> ## GH Test Kitchen Tip
> If you prefer firm slices, let the pie rest for at least twenty-five minutes before serving.

Sausage Calzones

These family favorites are stuffed with sausage and three kinds of cheese. The easy pizza dough recipe calls for quick-rise yeast, so no long rising period is needed.

⏱ **PREP** 45 minutes **BAKE** 30 to 35 minutes **MAKES** 4 main-dish servings

Calzone Dough (recipe follows)

8 ounces sweet or hot Italian-sausage links, casings removed

1 small onion, chopped

1 container (15 ounces) part-skim ricotta cheese

½ cup shredded part-skim mozzarella cheese

⅓ cup grated Parmesan cheese

1 tablespoon cornmeal

1. Prepare Calzone Dough.

2. While the dough is resting, prepare filling: In 10-inch skillet, cook sausage and onion over medium heat until browned, about 10 minutes, stirring to break up sausage. With slotted spoon, remove sausage mixture to large bowl. Stir in ricotta, mozzarella, and Parmesan until blended; set aside.

3. Preheat oven to 425°F. Sprinkle large cookie sheet with cornmeal.

4. Divide dough into 4 equal pieces. On lightly floured surface, with floured rolling pin, roll each piece of dough into a 7-inch round. Spoon about 1 cup filling onto half of each round, leaving ½-inch border. Fold the other half of dough over filling and pinch edges of dough together firmly. With 4-tine fork, press edges to seal.

5. Cut three 1½-inch slits in top of each calzone to allow steam to escape during baking. Place calzones on cookie sheet on bottom rack in oven. Bake 30 to 35 minutes, until golden. Serve hot.

CALZONE DOUGH In 1-cup glass measuring cup, dissolve **1 package quick-rise yeast** and **1 teaspoon sugar** in **1 cup warm water** (105° to 115°F.). Let yeast mixture stand about 5 minutes, until bubbly. In large bowl, mix **2¾ cups all-purpose flour** and **1 teaspoon salt**. With wooden spoon, stir in yeast mixture and **1 tablespoon olive oil** until dough pulls away from side of bowl; add ¼ **cup all-purpose flour** gradually to reduce stickiness if needed. Turn dough onto lightly floured surface and knead until smooth and elastic, about 5 to 7 minutes, adding more flour if needed. Shape dough into ball; cover and let rest 15 minutes.

EACH SERVING About 755 calories | 39 g protein | 84 g carbohydrate | 28 g total fat (13 g saturated) | 85 mg cholesterol | 1,320 mg sodium.

Chili Potpie with Cheddar-Biscuit Crust

The cornmeal-and-Cheddar crust adds an old-fashioned crowning touch to spicy beef chili—an irresistible combination.

PREP 30 minutes **BAKE** 1 hour 45 minutes to 2 hours **MAKES** 6 main-dish servings

1 tablespoon plus 3 teaspoons olive oil

1 pound boneless beef chuck, cut into ½-inch pieces

1 medium onion, chopped

2 garlic cloves, minced

1 tablespoon chili powder

1 teaspoon ground coriander

½ teaspoon salt

½ teaspoon ground cumin

1 can (16 ounces) whole tomatoes in puree

1 can (4 to 4½ ounces) chopped mild green chiles

1 tablespoon dark brown sugar

1 tablespoon tomato paste

1 can (15 to 16 ounces) pink beans

¼ cup chopped fresh cilantro leaves

Cheddar-Biscuit Crust (recipe follows)

2 teaspoons milk

green onions for garnish (optional)

1. In 5-quart Dutch oven or saucepot, heat 1 tablespoon olive oil over medium-high heat until hot. Add half the beef, and cook until browned and juices evaporate. Transfer beef to small bowl. Repeat with remaining beef and 2 teaspoons olive oil.

2. Add remaining 1 teaspoon olive oil to Dutch oven. Reduce heat to medium. Add onion and cook 10 minutes or until tender and golden. Add garlic; cook 2 minutes, stir-ring. Add chili powder, coriander, salt, and cumin; cook 1 minute, stirring.

3. Add tomatoes with their puree, breaking up tomatoes with side of spoon. Add chiles with their juice, brown sugar, tomato paste, beef with any accumulated juices in bowl, and ¼ *cup water*; heat to boiling over high heat. Reduce heat to low; cover and simmer 30 minutes, stirring occasionally.

4. Rinse and drain beans. Add beans; heat to boiling over high heat. Reduce heat to low; cover and simmer 30 to 45 minutes longer, until beef is very tender. Stir in cilantro.

5. Preheat oven to 425°F. Meanwhile, prepare Cheddar-Biscuit Crust.

6. Spoon hot chili mixture into deep 2-quart casserole or 9-inch deep-dish pie plate. Top with biscuit crust, tucking in edge to fit. With tip of knife, cut out 5 oval openings in crust to allow steam to escape during baking. (Do not just make slits, they will close up as crust bakes.) Brush crust with milk.

7. Place sheet of foil underneath casserole; crimp foil edges to form a rim to catch any drips during baking. Bake pie 20 minutes or until crust is browned. Cool slightly.

8. Garnish each serving with green onions if you like.

CHEDDAR-BISCUIT CRUST In a medium bowl, mix **1 cup all-purpose flour**, ⅓ **cup shredded sharp Cheddar cheese**, ¼ **cup yellow cornmeal, 2 teaspoons baking powder**, and ½ **teaspoon salt**. With pastry blender or 2 knives used scissor-fashion, cut in **3 tablespoons cold butter or margarine** until mixture resembles coarse crumbs. Stir in ½ **cup milk**; quickly mix just until a soft dough forms and leaves side of bowl. Turn dough onto lightly floured surface; gently knead about 5 strokes to mix thoroughly. With floured rolling pin, roll dough into a round 1 inch larger in diameter than top of casserole.

EACH SERVING About 515 calories | 24 g protein | 45 g carbohydrate | 27 g total fat (8 g saturated) | 58 mg cholesterol | 1,320 mg sodium.

Quiche Lorraine

This is the cheese and bacon quiche we all fell in love with. If you're pressed for time, use a refrigerated piecrust instead of the homemade pastry dough and bake as recipe directs.

PREP 35 minutes **BAKE** 55 minutes **MAKES** 8 main-dish servings

Pastry Dough for 1-Crust Pie (recipe follows)

4 slices bacon, chopped

4 large eggs

2 cups half-and-half or light cream

½ teaspoon salt

⅛ teaspoon ground black pepper

pinch ground nutmeg

4 ounces Gruyère or Swiss cheese, shredded (1 cup)

1. Prepare Pastry Dough for 1-Crust Pie. Preheat oven to 425°F. Use dough to line 9-inch pie plate. Line pie shell with foil and fill with pie weights or dry beans. Bake 10 minutes. Remove foil with weights; bake until golden, 5 to 10 minutes longer. Cool on wire rack. Turn oven control to 350°F.

2. Meanwhile, in 10-inch skillet, cook bacon over medium-low heat until browned. Transfer to paper towels to drain well.

3. In medium bowl, with wire whisk, beat eggs, half-and-half, salt, pepper, and nutmeg until well blended. Sprinkle bacon and Gruyère over bottom of crust; pour egg mixture over bacon and cheese.

4. Place pie plate on foil-lined cookie sheet to catch any overflow. Bake until knife inserted in center comes out clean, 55 to 60 minutes. Cool on wire rack 15 minutes. Serve hot or at room temperature.

EACH SERVING About 342 calories | 12 g protein | 18 g carbohydrate | 25 g total fat (13 g saturated) | 162 mg cholesterol | 429 mg sodium.

PASTRY DOUGH In large bowl, combine **1¼ cups all-purpose flour** and ¼ **teaspoon salt**. With pastry blender or 2 knives used scissor-fashion, cut in **4 tablespoons cold butter or margarine,** cut into pieces and **2 tablespoons vegetable shortening** until mixture resembles coarse crumbs. Sprinkle in **3 to 5 tablespoons ice water**, 1 tablespoon at a time, mixing lightly with fork after each addition, until dough is just moist enough to hold together. Shape dough into disk; wrap in plastic wrap. Refrigerate 30 minutes or up to overnight. (If chilled overnight, let stand 30 minutes at room temperature before rolling.) On lightly floured surface, with floured rolling pin, roll dough into 12-inch round. Ease into pie plate, gently pressing dough against side of plate. Make decorative edge as desired. Refrigerate or freeze until firm, 10 to 15 minutes. Fill and bake as directed in recipe. Makes enough dough for one 9-inch crust.

Sherried Crab Quiche

Prepare and bake Pastry Dough for 1-Crust Pie. Prepare egg mixture as directed but omit bacon and Gruyère. In 1-quart saucepan, melt **1 tablespoon butter or margarine** over medium heat; add **2 tablespoons chopped green onions**. Cook until tender, about 5 minutes. Stir **8 ounces crabmeat**, picked over, green onions, **2 tablespoons dry sherry**, **¼ teaspoon salt**, and **⅛ teaspoon ground red pepper (cayenne)** into egg mixture. Pour into piecrust. Proceed with Step 4.

EACH SERVING About 313 calories | 13 g protein | 18 g carbohydrate | 20 g total fat (10 g saturated) | 176 mg cholesterol | 497 mg sodium.

Mushroom Quiche

Prepare and bake Pastry Dough for 1-Crust Pie. Prepare egg mixture as directed but omit bacon and Gruyère. In 10-inch skillet, melt **2 tablespoons butter or margarine** over medium-high heat; add **8 ounces mushrooms**, trimmed and very thinly sliced, **2 tablespoons finely chopped onion**, **¼ teaspoon salt**, **⅛ teaspoon coarsely ground black pepper**, and **pinch dried thyme**. Cook, stirring frequently, until mushrooms are tender and liquid has evaporated, about 10 minutes. Add to egg mixture, stirring to mix. Pour into piecrust. Proceed with Step 4, but reduce baking time to 45 to 50 minutes.

EACH SERVING About 299 calories | 8 g protein | 19 g carbohydrate | 22 g total fat (11 g saturated) | 152 mg cholesterol | 433 mg sodium.

Asparagus Quiche

Prepare and bake Pastry Dough for 1-Crust Pie. Prepare egg mixture as directed but omit bacon. Trim **1 pound asparagus** and cut into ¾-inch pieces (2½ cups). In 2-quart saucepan, heat **4 cups water** to boiling over high heat. Add asparagus and cook until tender, 6 to 8 minutes; drain. Rinse asparagus with cold running water; drain. Spread asparagus over bottom of crust and sprinkle with Gruyère; pour egg mixture over. Proceed with Step 4, but reduce baking time to 40 to 45 minutes.

EACH SERVING About 334 calories | 13 g protein | 20 g carbohydrate | 23 g total fat (12 g saturated) | 160 mg cholesterol | 380 mg sodium.

Savory Tomato Tart

A dramatically beautiful main dish. We used a yellow tomato for more color, but you can use all red if you prefer.

PREP 45 minutes **BAKE/BROIL** about 30 minutes **MAKES** 6 main-dish servings

Pastry for 11-inch Tart (recipe follows)

1 tablespoon olive oil

3 medium onions, thinly sliced

$\frac{1}{2}$ teaspoon salt

1 package (3$\frac{1}{2}$ ounces) goat cheese

1 ripe medium yellow tomato (8 ounces), cut into $\frac{1}{4}$-inch-thick slices

2 ripe medium red tomatoes (8 ounces each), cut into $\frac{1}{4}$-inch-thick slices

$\frac{1}{2}$ teaspoon coarsely ground black pepper

$\frac{1}{4}$ cup kalamata olives, pitted and chopped

1. Preheat oven to 425°F. Prepare Pastry for 11-inch Tart and use to line tart pan as directed. Line tart shell with foil; fill with pie weights or dry beans. Bake 15 minutes. Remove foil with weights. Bake until golden, 5 to 10 minutes longer. If shell puffs up during baking, gently press it down with back of spoon.

2. Meanwhile, in nonstick 12-inch skillet, heat oil over medium heat. Add onions and $\frac{1}{4}$ teaspoon salt; cook, stirring frequently, until very tender, about 20 minutes.

3. Turn oven control to broil. Spread onions over bottom of tart shell and crumble half of goat cheese on top. Arrange yellow and red tomatoes, alternating colors, in concentric circles over onion-cheese mixture. Sprinkle with remaining $\frac{1}{4}$ teaspoon salt and ground pepper. Crumble remaining goat cheese on top of tart.

4. Place tart on rack in broiling pan. Place pan in broiler about 7 inches from heat source. Broil until cheese has melted and tomatoes are heated through, 6 to 8 minutes. Sprinkle with olives.

PASTRY FOR 11-INCH TART In large bowl, combine 1$\frac{1}{2}$ **cups all-purpose flour** and $\frac{1}{2}$ **teaspoon salt.** With pastry blender or 2 knives used scissor-fashion, cut in $\frac{1}{2}$ **cup cold butter or margarine (1 stick),** cut into pieces and **2 tablespoons vegetable shortening** until mixture resembles coarse crumbs. Sprinkle in **3 to 4 tablespoons ice water,** 1 tablespoon at a time, mixing lightly with fork after each addition, until dough is just moist enough to hold together. Shape dough into disk; wrap in plastic wrap. Refrigerate 30 minutes or up to overnight. (If chilled overnight, let stand 30 minutes at room temperature before rolling.) On lightly floured surface, with floured rolling pin, roll dough into 14-inch round. Ease dough into 11-inch tart pan with removable bottom. Fold overhang in and press dough against side of pan so it extends $\frac{1}{8}$ inch above rim. Refrigerate or freeze until firm, 10 to 15 minutes. Fill and bake as directed in recipe.

EACH SERVING About 420 calories | 8 g protein | 33 g carbohydrate | 29 g total fat (15 g saturated) | 54 mg cholesterol | 755 mg sodium.

Couscous Paella

A box of couscous makes paella quick enough for a weeknight. You can substitute chorizo sausage for the kielbasa.

🕐 PREP 10 minutes COOK 10 minutes MAKES 4 main-dish servings

1 can (14½ ounces) chicken broth

1 package (10 ounces) couscous (1½ cups)

1 package (10 ounces) frozen peas

2 teaspoons olive oil

1 red or green pepper, diced

2 ounces low-fat kielbasa (smoked Polish sausage), sliced

12 ounces skinless, boneless chicken breast, cut into 1-inch pieces

1 garlic clove, crushed with garlic press

½ teaspoon salt

¼ teaspoon dried thyme

¼ teaspoon coarsely ground black pepper

1½ cups cherry tomatoes, each cut in half

1. In 3-quart saucepan, heat chicken broth and ¼ *cup water* to boiling over high heat. Remove saucepan from heat; stir in couscous and frozen peas. Cover saucepan and let stand 5 minutes or until ready to use.

2. Meanwhile, in nonstick 12-inch skillet, heat olive oil over medium-high heat until hot. Add red or green pepper and kielbasa and cook 5 minutes, stirring occasionally. Add chicken, garlic, salt, thyme, and black pepper, and cook until chicken loses its pink color throughout, about 5 minutes, stirring occasionally. Remove skillet from heat and stir in cherry-tomato halves.

3. Fluff the couscous with fork; add to the chicken mixture in skillet, and toss gently until combined.

EACH SERVING About 520 calories | 38 g protein | 73 g carbohydrate | 8 g total fat (1 g saturated) | 50 mg cholesterol | 725 mg sodium.

Turkey Potpie with Cornmeal Crust

Treat your family to the ultimate in comfort food—tender turkey and veggies in a velvety sauce nestled under a golden crust.

🕐 **PREP** 30 minutes **BAKE** 35 minutes **MAKES** 10 main-dish servings

1 tablespoon vegetable oil

1 medium rutabaga (1 pound), peeled and cut into ½-inch pieces

3 carrots, peeled and cut into ½-inch pieces

1 large onion (12 ounces), chopped

1 pound all-purpose potatoes (3 medium), peeled and cut into ½-inch pieces

2 large stalks celery, chopped

¾ teaspoon salt

1 pound cooked turkey or chicken, cut into ½-inch pieces (4 cups)

1 package (10 ounces) frozen peas

1 can (14½ ounces) chicken broth or 1¾ cups Chicken Broth (page 9)

1 cup milk

¼ cup all-purpose flour

¼ teaspoon ground black pepper

⅛ teaspoon dried thyme

Cornmeal Crust (recipe follows)

1 large egg, beaten

1. In nonstick 12-inch skillet, heat oil over medium-high heat; add rutabaga, carrots, and onion and cook 10 minutes. Stir in potatoes, celery, and ½ teaspoon salt; cook, stirring frequently, until rutabaga is tender-crisp, about 10 minutes longer. Spoon into 13" by 9" baking dish; add turkey and peas.

2. In 2-quart saucepan, heat broth to boiling. Meanwhile, in small bowl, blend milk and flour until smooth. Stir milk mixture into broth; add pepper, thyme, and remaining ¼ teaspoon salt. Heat to boiling over high heat, stirring. Stir sauce into turkey-vegetable mixture in baking dish.

3. Prepare the Cornmeal Crust. Preheat oven to 425°F.

4. On lightly floured surface, with floured rolling pin, roll dough into rectangle 4 inches larger than top of baking dish. Arrange dough rectangle over filling; trim edge, leaving 1-inch overhang. Fold overhang under; flute. Brush crust with some egg. If desired, reroll trimmings; cut into decorative shapes to garnish top of pie. Brush dough cutouts with egg. Cut several slits in crust to allow steam to escape during baking.

5. Place potpie on foil-lined cookie sheet to catch any overflow during baking. Bake potpie until crust is golden brown and filling is hot and bubbling, 35 to 40 minutes. During last 10 minutes of baking, cover edges of crust with foil to prevent overbrowning.

CORNMEAL CRUST In large bowl, combine **1½ cups all-purpose flour, ¼ cup cornmeal,** and **¾ teaspoon salt**. With pastry blender or 2 knives used scissor-fashion, cut in ⅔ **cup vegetable shortening** until mixture resembles coarse crumbs. Sprinkle **6 to 7 tablespoons cold water**, 1 tablespoon at a time, over flour mixture, mixing with fork after each addition until dough is just moist enough to hold together.

EACH SERVING About 416 calories | 21 g protein | 42 g carbohydrate | 18 g total fat (5 g saturated) | 60 mg cholesterol | 644 mg sodium.

Tuna-Melt Casserole

If you enjoy diner tuna-melt sandwiches, you'll love this. We've added tomatoes and broccoli for flavor, color, and vitamins.

PREP 40 minutes   **BAKE** 20 minutes   **MAKES** 6 main-dish servings

1 package (16 ounces) corkscrew or medium shell pasta

salt

3 cups broccoli flowerets

2 tablespoons butter or margarine

2 tablespoons all-purpose flour

¼ teaspoon coarsely ground black pepper

4 cups reduced-fat (2%) milk

4 ounces Swiss cheese, shredded (1 cup)

1 can (12 ounces) chunk light tuna in water, drained and flaked

2 medium tomatoes, cut into ¼-inch-thick slices

1. Preheat oven to 400°F. In large saucepot, cook pasta in *boiling salted water* 5 minutes; add broccoli to pasta and cook another 5 minutes or until broccoli is tender and pasta is al dente. Drain well and return to saucepot; set aside.

2. Meanwhile, in 3-quart saucepan, melt butter over low heat. Stir in flour, ¾ teaspoon salt, and pepper until blended and cook, stirring, 1 minute. Gradually stir in milk; increase heat to medium-high and cook, stirring occasionally, until mixture thickens and boils. Boil 1 minute, stirring frequently. Remove saucepan from heat and stir in ½ cup Swiss cheese until blended.

3. Add cheese sauce and tuna to pasta and broccoli in saucepot; toss until evenly mixed. Transfer mixture to shallow 3½-quart casserole or 13" by 9" glass baking dish. Arrange tomato slices on top, overlapping if necessary. Sprinkle with remaining ½ cup cheese.

4. Cover baking dish with foil and bake 20 minutes or until hot and bubbly.

EACH SERVING About 570 calories | 39 g protein | 71 g carbohydrate | 14 g total fat (6 g saturated) | 29 mg cholesterol | 755 mg sodium.

Linguine with Tuna and Broccoli

In our delicious new variation on linguine with clam sauce, we have tuna cooked with garlic and white wine stand in for the clams.

PREP 5 minutes   **COOK** 10 minutes   **MAKES** 4 main-dish servings

2 packages (9 ounces each) fresh (refrigerated) linguine

2 packages (10 ounces each) frozen broccoli cuts

salt

2 tablespoons olive oil

3 garlic cloves, crushed with garlic press

¼ teaspoon crushed red pepper

¼ cup dry white wine

1 can (12 ounces) tuna packed in water, drained and flaked

1. In large saucepot, heat *5 quarts water* to boiling over high heat. Add pasta, broccoli, and 2 teaspoons salt; cook 2 to 3 minutes or until linguine and broccoli are tender.

2. Meanwhile, in nonstick 10-inch skillet, heat oil over medium-high heat until hot. Add garlic and crushed red pepper, and cook 1 minute, stirring. Add wine and heat to boiling; boil 1 minute, stirring. Stir in tuna and cook 30 seconds.

3. When linguine is cooked, remove *½ cup pasta cooking water*; reserve. Drain linguine and broccoli and return to saucepot. Add tuna mixture, ½ teaspoon salt, and reserved pasta cooking water; toss until well mixed.

EACH SERVING About 595 calories | 36 g protein | 79 g carbohydrate | 15 g total fat (3 g saturated) | 174 mg cholesterol | 800 mg sodium.

Thai Pasta with Shrimp

Delicate angel hair pasta absorbs sauce quickly, so put this on plates as soon as it's tossed. Serve with lime wedges if you like.

 PREP 15 minutes   COOK 15 minutes   MAKES 6 main-dish servings

1 package (16 ounces) angel hair pasta

salt

2 teaspoons curry powder

1 can (14 ounces) light coconut milk (not cream of coconut)

1/8 teaspoon coarsely ground black pepper

1 pound medium shrimp, shelled and deveined with tail part of shell left on (see page 11)

1 cup loosely packed fresh cilantro leaves

1. In large saucepot, prepare pasta in *boiling salted water* as label directs.

2. Meanwhile, in 10-inch skillet, cook curry powder over medium heat 2 minutes, stirring frequently. Stir in coconut milk, 1 teaspoon salt, and 1/8 teaspoon ground black pepper until blended; heat to boiling over high heat. Add shrimp; reduce heat to medium. Cover and cook 2 minutes or until shrimp just turn opaque throughout.

3. Drain pasta. In large bowl, toss pasta with shrimp mixture and cilantro.

EACH SERVING About 410 calories | 23 g protein | 59 g carbohydrate | 8 g total fat (4 g saturated) | 95 mg cholesterol | 550 mg sodium.

Greek Pasta Bowl with Shrimp

Oregano and feta cheese—two staples of Greek cooking—flavor this dish. For an even speedier prep time, substitute pre-shelled and deveined frozen raw shrimp for the fresh.

PREP 15 minutes **COOK** about 15 minutes **MAKES** 6 main-dish servings

salt

1 package (16 ounces) gemelli or fusilli pasta

2 tablespoons olive oil

1 pound medium shrimp, shelled and deveined (see page 11)

2 garlic cloves, crushed with garlic press

1 tablespoon fresh oregano leaves, minced, or ½ teaspoon dried oregano

¼ teaspoon ground black pepper

2 bunches green onions, thinly sliced

3 medium tomatoes (about 1 pound), coarsely chopped

2 packages (4 ounces each) crumbled feta cheese (about 2 cups)

fresh oregano sprigs for garnish

1. Heat large saucepot of *salted water* to boiling over high heat. Add pasta and cook as label directs.

2. Meanwhile, in nonstick 12-inch skillet, heat oil over medium-high heat until hot. Add shrimp, garlic, oregano, pepper, and ½ teaspoon salt, and cook 1 minute, stirring. Add green onions and cook 2 minutes or just until shrimp turn opaque throughout. Stir in tomatoes.

3. Drain pasta; return to saucepot. Add shrimp mixture and feta; toss well to combine. Garnish each serving with the fresh oregano sprigs.

EACH SERVING About 515 calories | 29 g protein | 65 g carbohydrate | 15 g total fat (7 g saturated) | 127 mg cholesterol | 815 mg sodium.

Caramelized Onion and Goat Cheese Tart

A salad of baby greens is the perfect foil for this cheese-studded tart.

⏱ **PREP** 1 hour 15 minutes **BAKE** about 1 hour **MAKES** 6 main-dish servings

CRUST

1½ cups all-purpose flour

½ teaspoon salt

¼ cup vegetable shortening

4 tablespoons cold butter or margarine, cut up

4 tablespoons cold water

ONION AND GOAT CHEESE FILLING

1 tablespoon olive oil

1 tablespoon butter or margarine

2 jumbo onions (1 pound each), each cut lengthwise in half, then cut crosswise into thin slices

½ teaspoon salt

¼ teaspoon coarsely ground black pepper

3 large eggs

1 cup milk

⅔ cup half-and-half or light cream

1 package (3 to 4 ounces) mild goat cheese, such as Montrachet, crumbled

¼ cup loosely packed fresh parsley leaves, chopped

SALAD

1 tablespoon olive oil

2 teaspoons seasoned rice vinegar

2 teaspoons balsamic vinegar

¼ teaspoon Dijon mustard

⅛ teaspoon salt

⅛ teaspoon coarsely ground black pepper

6 ounces mixed baby greens (about 10 cups)

1. Prepare Crust: In medium bowl, with wire whisk or fork, stir flour and salt. With pastry blender or 2 knives used scissor-fashion, cut in shortening with butter until mixture resembles coarse crumbs. Sprinkle water, 1 tablespoon at a time, into flour mixture, mixing lightly with fork after each addition until mixture is just moist enough to hold together. With hands, shape dough into a disk.

2. Preheat oven to 425°F. On lightly floured surface, with floured rolling pin, roll dough into 14-inch round. Press dough onto bottom and up side of 11" by 1" tart pan with removable bottom. Fold overhang in and press against side of tart pan to form a rim ⅛ inch above edge of pan. With fork, prick dough at 1-inch intervals to prevent puffing and shrinking during baking.

3. Line tart shell with foil and fill with pie weights, dry beans, or uncooked rice. Bake 15 minutes; remove foil with weights and bake 15 minutes longer or until golden. If crust puffs up during baking, gently press it to tart pan with back of spoon. Remove tart shell from oven; cool on wire rack. Turn oven control to 400°F.

4. While tart shell is baking, prepare Onion and Goat Cheese filling: In nonstick 12-inch skillet, heat olive oil with butter over medium heat. Add onions, salt, and pepper and cook 25 to 30 minutes, until onions are golden, stirring occasionally. Stir in *2 tablespoons water* during last minute of cooking time.

5. In medium bowl, with wire whisk or fork, mix eggs, milk, and half-and-half until blended.

6. Place onions in tart shell. Pour egg mixture over onions. Bake 25 to 30 minutes, until filling is set and lightly browned. Top tart with crumbled goat cheese and bake 3 minutes longer. Transfer tart to wire rack; let stand 10 minutes to serve hot. Or, cool tart on wire rack to serve at room temperature later.

7. While tart is baking, prepare Salad: In small bowl, with wire whisk or fork, mix olive oil, both vinegars, mustard, salt, and pepper until blended. Or, place vinaigrette ingredients in small jar and shake to blend.

8. To serve, in large bowl, toss greens with vinaigrette. Sprinkle tart with parsley; cut tart into 10 wedges. Serve each wedge with some of the salad.

EACH SERVING About 533 calories | 15 g protein | 43 g carbohydrate | 33 g total fat (12 g saturated) | 130 mg cholesterol | 800 mg sodium.

GH Test Kitchen Tip

If you can't find mild goat cheese, use ⅓ cup freshly grated Parmesan instead.

Mushroom Lasagna

In northern Italy, lasagna is traditionally made with creamy béchamel sauce.

PREP 1 hour plus standing **BAKE** 50 minutes **MAKES** 12 main-dish servings

½ ounce dried porcini mushrooms

¾ (16-ounce) package lasagna noodles
  (about 16 noodles)

5 cups milk

5 tablespoons butter or margarine

⅓ cup all-purpose flour

pinch ground nutmeg

salt

ground black pepper

½ cup finely chopped shallots

1½ pounds white mushrooms, sliced

2 tablespoons chopped fresh parsley

1 container (15 ounces) ricotta cheese

1 package (10 ounces) frozen chopped spinach,
  thawed and squeezed dry

1 cup freshly grated Parmesan cheese

1. In bowl, combine porcini and *¾ cup hot water*; let stand 30 minutes. With slotted spoon, remove porcini; rinse to remove any grit. Chop and set aside. Strain mushroom soaking liquid through sieve lined with paper towel; set aside. Meanwhile, prepare lasagna noodles as label directs, but do not add salt to water; drain and rinse with cold running water. Return noodles to saucepot with *cold water* to cover. Set aside.

2. Prepare béchamel sauce: In 3-quart saucepan, heat milk to boiling over medium-high heat. Meanwhile, in 4-quart saucepan, melt 3 tablespoons butter or margarine over medium heat. Stir in flour; cook, stirring, for 1 minute. Gradually whisk in the hot milk, nutmeg, ½ teaspoon salt, and ⅛ teaspoon pepper; heat to boiling. Reduce heat to low; simmer 5 minutes, stirring.

3. In 12-inch skillet, melt remaining 2 tablespoons butter over medium-high heat. Add shallots; cook 1 minute. Stir in white mushrooms, ½ teaspoon salt, and ⅛ teaspoon pepper and cook 10 minutes or until liquid has evaporated. Stir in porcini and soaking liquid; cook until liquid has evaporated. Remove skillet from heat; stir in parsley.

4. Preheat oven to 375°F. In large bowl, mix ricotta, spinach, ¼ cup Parmesan, ½ teaspoon salt, ¼ teaspoon pepper, and ½ cup béchamel. Drain noodles on clean kitchen towels.

5. In 13" by 9" glass baking dish, spread ½ cup béchamel. Arrange 4 lasagna noodles over sauce, overlapping slightly. Top with half of mushroom mixture, 1 cup béchamel, ¼ cup Parmesan, and 4 more noodles. Add all of ricotta mixture, 4 more noodles, remaining mushrooms, 1 cup béchamel, and ¼ cup Parmesan. Top with remaining noodles, béchamel, and Parmesan. Cover with foil; bake 30 minutes.

6. Uncover dish and bake lasagna 20 minutes longer, or until sauce is hot and bubbly and top is lightly browned. Remove lasagna from oven and let stand 15 minutes for easier serving.

EACH SERVING About 355 calories | 18 g protein | 36 g carbohydrate | 16 g total fat (8 g saturated) | 38 mg cholesterol | 580 mg sodium.

Fettuccine with Creamy Tomato Sauce and Peas

With quick-cooking fresh pasta and an almost instant sauce, you can have a home-cooked meal on the table in about fifteen minutes.

PREP 5 minutes   **COOK** 10 minutes   **MAKES** 4 main-dish servings

2 packages (9 ounces each) fresh (refrigerated) fettuccine

2 teaspoons salt

1 can (14½ ounces) seasoned chunky tomatoes for pasta

1 can (15 ounces) tomato sauce

⅓ cup heavy or whipping cream

1 package (10 ounces) frozen peas

grated Parmesan cheese (optional)

1. In large saucepot, heat *5 quarts water* to boiling over high heat. Add pasta and salt; cook as label directs.

2. Meanwhile, in 2-quart saucepan, heat tomatoes, tomato sauce, and cream to boiling over medium-high heat. Reduce heat to medium and cook 2 minutes, stirring.

3. Place frozen peas in colander. Drain fettuccine over peas. In large serving bowl, toss fettuccine and peas with tomato mixture. Serve with Parmesan if you like.

EACH SERVING About 575 calories | 22 g protein | 96 g carbohydrate | 13 g total fat (6 g saturated) | 158 mg cholesterol | 1,375 mg sodium.

Potato Dumplings with Cabbage and Apples

Pierogi—Polish-style comfort food—are usually filled with meat, seafood, cheese, potatoes, or mushrooms. They can be quite time-consuming to make, but fortunately, excellent frozen varieties are available. Serve with pumpernickel-raisin rolls and a sliced tomato salad.

PREP 5 minutes   **COOK** 25 minutes   **MAKES** 4 main-dish servings

1 package (16 to 19 ounces) frozen potato-
   and-onion pierogi

salt

1 tablespoon butter or margarine

1 small onion, thinly sliced

1½ pounds green cabbage (1 small head),
   sliced, with tough ribs discarded

½ cup chicken broth

2 medium McIntosh apples (about 12 ounces)

2 teaspoons cider vinegar

1 tablespoon chopped fresh dill

1. In large saucepot, prepare pierogi in *boiling salted water* as label directs.

2. Meanwhile, in nonstick 12-inch skillet, melt butter over medium-low heat. Add onion to skillet and cook, stirring occasionally, 7 minutes or until onion is tender and lightly browned.

3. Increase heat to medium-high; add cabbage, chicken broth, and ½ teaspoon salt and cook until cabbage is tender, about 10 minutes. While cabbage is cooking, core and cut apples into ¼-inch-thick wedges.

4. Add apples and vinegar to skillet with cabbage mixture and cook until apples soften, about 5 minutes.

5. Drain pierogi; toss with cabbage mixture and chopped dill.

EACH SERVING About 355 calories | 9 g protein | 64 g carbohydrate | 7 g total fat (2 g saturated) | 0 mg cholesterol | 950 mg sodium.

Fettuccine with Mushrooms and Cream

Why go out for pasta when you can whip up this elegant yet hearty dish in your own kitchen in just minutes?

PREP 15 minutes **COOK** about 15 minutes **MAKES** 4 main-dish servings

salt

2 packages (9 ounces each) fresh (refrigerated) fettuccine pasta

1 tablespoon olive oil

1 small shallot, finely chopped (2 tablespoons)

8 ounces shiitake mushrooms, stems removed, caps thinly sliced

8 ounces white mushrooms, thinly sliced

¼ cup Marsala wine

1½ cups chicken broth

⅓ cup heavy or whipping cream

1 cup loosely packed fresh basil or parsley leaves, chopped

¼ cup sun-dried tomatoes in olive oil, sliced

1. Heat large saucepot of *salted water* to boiling over high heat. Add fettuccine and cook as label directs.

2. Meanwhile, in nonstick 12-inch skillet, heat oil over medium-high heat until hot. Add shallot and cook 1 minute, stirring occasionally. Add mushrooms and ½ teaspoon salt and cook 10 to 12 minutes or until tender and golden, stirring occasionally.

3. Stir wine into mushroom mixture. Heat to boiling and cook 1 minute. Add chicken broth and cream; heat to boiling and cook 3 minutes, stirring.

4. Drain fettuccine and return to saucepot. Add mushroom mixture, basil, and sun-dried tomatoes, and cook 1 minute over medium heat, tossing until evenly coated.

EACH SERVING About 560 calories | 20 g protein | 83 g carbohydrate | 18 g total fat (7 g saturated) | 158 mg cholesterol | 815 mg sodium.

Salads & Sandwiches

Falafel Sandwiches

Panfried Steak and Onions on Grilled Bread

The green herb sauce is a natural with grilled meat. Afghan flatbread is a good alternative to Italian-style flatbreads.

⏱ **PREP** 40 minutes   **COOK** 30 minutes   **MAKES** 6 sandwiches

PANFRIED STEAK AND ONIONS

2 teaspoons olive oil

1 beef flank steak (1½ pounds)

¼ teaspoon coarsely ground black pepper

¾ teaspoon salt

2 large red onions, thinly sliced

HERB SAUCE

1 cup loosely packed fresh parsley leaves, chopped

1 cup loosely packed fresh cilantro leaves, chopped

3 tablespoons olive oil

2 tablespoons red wine vinegar

¼ teaspoon salt

¼ teaspoon coarsely ground black pepper

pinch crushed red pepper

1 small garlic clove, crushed with garlic press

2 Italian-style grilled flatbreads (one 13½-ounce package) or 1 Afghan flatbread (16 ounces), cut crosswise in half, warmed

1. Prepare panfried steak and onions: In heavy 12-inch skillet (preferably cast iron), heat olive oil over high heat until very hot. Meanwhile, sprinkle flank steak with pepper and ½ teaspoon salt.

2. Add steak to hot skillet; reduce heat to medium-high and cook 12 to 17 minutes for medium-rare (depending on thickness of meat) or until of desired doneness, turning once. Transfer steak to cutting board.

3. Reduce heat to medium. Add onions and remaining ¼ teaspoon salt and cook until tender and browned, 12 to 15 minutes, stirring occasionally.

4. While onions are cooking, prepare herb sauce: In small bowl, mix parsley, cilantro, olive oil, vinegar, salt, black pepper, crushed red pepper, and garlic; set aside.

5. To serve, thinly slice flank steak. Drizzle 1 flatbread with 2 tablespoons herb sauce; top with steak slices, onion slices, 2 tablespoons herb sauce, then remaining flatbread. Cut sandwich into 6 pieces. Pass remaining sauce to serve with sandwiches.

EACH SANDWICH About 490 calories | 29 g protein | 46 g carbohydrate | 20 g total fat (6 g saturated) | 58 mg cholesterol | 635 mg sodium.

Philly Cheese Steaks

These sandwiches have all the flavor of the traditional Philadelphia treat but take half the time. To streamline prep, we broil the buns and beef while the onions and peppers cook on the stovetop.

⏱ **PREP** 10 minutes   **COOK** 12 minutes   **MAKES** 4 sandwiches

1 teaspoon olive oil

1 jumbo onion (12 ounces), thinly sliced

1 medium red pepper, thinly sliced

1 medium green pepper, thinly sliced

4 hero-style rolls (about 3 ounces each), each cut horizontally in half

8 ounces thinly sliced deli roast beef

4 ounces thinly sliced Provolone cheese

1. In nonstick 12-inch skillet, heat olive oil over medium-high heat until hot. Add onion and peppers, and cook about 12 minutes or until tender and golden, stirring the mixture occasionally.

2. Meanwhile, preheat broiler. Place rolls, cut sides up, on rack in broiling pan. Top each bottom half with one-fourth of roast beef and one-fourth of cheese. With broiling pan 5 to 7 inches from source of heat, broil 1 to 2 minutes, until the cheese melts and the bread is toasted.

3. Pile onion mixture on top of melted cheese; replace top halves of rolls.

EACH SANDWICH About 620 calories | 35 g protein | 60 g carbohydrate | 26 g total fat (12 g saturated) | 94 mg cholesterol | 500 mg sodium.

Beef and Pepper Fajitas

We seasoned a flank steak with a spicy rub before searing it in a grill pan for these tasty Mexican wraps.

PREP 30 minutes   **COOK** about 20 minutes   **MAKES** 6 main-dish servings

2 limes

I garlic clove, crushed with garlic press

2 tablespoons plus ¾ teaspoon chili powder

I tablespoon plus ½ teaspoon brown sugar

¾ teaspoon salt

I beef flank steak (about I pound), trimmed

2 teaspoons olive oil

I large red pepper, thinly sliced

I large green pepper, thinly sliced

I large red onion, cut in half and thinly sliced

6 burrito-size flour tortillas, warmed

accompaniments: salsa, light sour cream, cilantro leaves (optional)

I. From limes, grate 1 teaspoon peel and squeeze 2 tablespoons plus 1 teaspoon juice.

2. In large bowl, mix garlic, lime peel, 2 tablespoons lime juice, 2 tablespoons chili powder, 1 tablespoon sugar, and ½ teaspoon salt until blended. Add steak to bowl and rub all over with chili-powder mixture. Marinate steak 15 minutes at room temperature or up to 1 hour in the refrigerator.

3. Heat grill pan over medium-high heat until hot. Add steak and cook 20 to 25 minutes for medium-rare or until of desired doneness, turning steak over once (reduce heat to medium if steak browns too quickly).

4. Meanwhile, in nonstick 12-inch skillet, heat oil over medium heat until hot. Add peppers and onion and cook covered, 10 minutes, stirring occasionally. Add remaining ¾ teaspoon chili powder, ½ teaspoon sugar, and ¼ teaspoon salt, and cook 5 minutes longer, uncovered, or until vegetables are tender and golden, stirring occasionally. Stir in remaining 1 teaspoon lime juice.

5. Transfer steak to cutting board; let stand 10 minutes to allow juices to set for easier slicing. Thinly slice steak and wrap in tortillas with pepper mixture. Serve with salsa, sour cream, and cilantro if you like.

EACH SERVING WITHOUT ACCOMPANIMENTS About 310 calories | 23 g protein | 36g carbohydrate | 9 g total fat (3 g saturated) | 31 mg cholesterol | 710 mg sodium.

Taco Salad

Better than a taco! For quick assembly, have all the ingredients chopped and ready to go.

⏲ PREP 30 minutes   COOK 20 minutes   MAKES 6 main-dish servings

2 teaspoons vegetable oil

I medium onion, chopped

I garlic clove, finely chopped

2 tablespoons chili powder

I teaspoon ground cumin

I pound ground beef chuck

I can (8 ounces) tomato sauce

I head iceberg lettuce, cut into quarters,
   cored, and very thinly sliced

I large ripe tomato (10 ounces), finely
   chopped

I ripe avocado, peeled, pitted, and chopped

4 ounces sharp Cheddar cheese, shredded
   (I cup)

3 tablespoons sour cream

I cup loosely packed small cilantro leaves

½ bag (5 ounces) tortilla chips

1. In 10-inch skillet, heat oil over medium heat. Add onion and cook, stirring occasionally, until tender, about 5 minutes. Stir in garlic, chili powder, and cumin and cook 30 seconds. Add ground beef, stirring to break up lumps with side of spoon; cook until no longer pink, about 5 minutes. Stir in tomato sauce and cook 5 minutes longer.

2. Divide lettuce among dinner plates. Spoon warm beef mixture on top of lettuce. Sprinkle with tomato, avocado, and Cheddar. Top each with some sour cream; sprinkle with cilantro. Tuck tortilla chips around edge of each plate.

EACH SERVING About 506 calories | 22 g protein | 21 g carbohydrate | 38 g total fat (15 g saturated) | 87 mg cholesterol | 504 mg sodium.

GH Test Kitchen Tip

For a heartier dish, add drained canned beans or corn to the beef mixture.

Fried-Green-Tomato Sandwiches

Here's a BLT, southern style. Instead of regular mayonnaise, we blended low-fat mayo, plain yogurt, chives, and black pepper—it's so good you may want to try it on all your sandwiches.

PREP 10 minutes   COOK 20 minutes   MAKES 4 sandwiches

1 package (8 ounces) sliced bacon

1 large egg white

¼ teaspoon salt

½ cup cornmeal

½ teaspoon coarsely ground black pepper

1 pound green tomatoes (3 medium), cut into ½-inch-thick slices

¼ cup low-fat mayonnaise

¼ cup low-fat plain yogurt

2 tablespoons chopped fresh chives

8 slices firm whole-grain or white bread, toasted

4 green-leaf lettuce leaves

1. In 12-inch skillet, cook bacon over medium heat until browned. Remove bacon to paper towels to drain.

2. Meanwhile, in pie plate, beat egg white and salt. In another pie plate or on waxed paper, combine cornmeal and ¼ teaspoon pepper. Dip tomato slices in egg-white mixture to coat both sides, then dip into cornmeal mixture to coat both sides well. Place coated slices on waxed paper.

3. In drippings in skillet, cook tomato slices, a few at a time, over medium-high heat until golden brown on both sides and heated through, about 3 minutes. Drain tomatoes on paper towels.

4. In small bowl, combine mayonnaise, yogurt, chives, and ¼ teaspoon pepper.

5. Spread mayonnaise mixture on 1 side of toast slices. Arrange lettuce, tomatoes, then bacon on 4 toast slices; top with remaining toast slices, mayonnaise side down.

EACH SANDWICH About 430 calories | 14 g protein | 48 g carbohydrate | 21 g total fat (7 g saturated) | 23 mg cholesterol | 885 mg sodium.

Muffuletta

This savory meat and cheese sandwich with olives is a classic in the French Quarter of New Orleans, but with our recipe you won't have to travel to get it. The name comes from the Italian muffuliette, which refers to soft Sicilian rolls. The first muffuletta was served at Central Grocery Company, and serious sandwich fans claim it still serves the best.

 PREP 30 minutes plus chilling MAKES 8 main-dish servings

4 medium stalks celery, finely chopped (about 1¼ cups)

1 cup drained giardiniera (Italian mixed pickled vegetables), finely chopped

1 cup loosely packed fresh parsley leaves, chopped

¾ cup pitted green olives, finely chopped

¼ cup olive oil

¼ teaspoon coarsely ground black pepper

1 garlic clove, minced

1 round (10-inch-diameter) loaf soft French or Italian bread (1 pound), cut horizontally in half

6 ounces thinly sliced smoked ham

6 ounces thinly sliced provolone cheese

6 ounces thinly sliced Genoa salami

1. In medium bowl, combine celery, giardiniera, parsley, olives, oil, pepper, and garlic; set aside.

2. Remove a 1-inch layer of soft center of bread from both halves to make room for filling. On bottom half of bread, spread half of olive mixture; top with ham, cheese, salami, and remaining olive mixture. Replace top half of bread; press halves together.

3. Wrap sandwich tightly in plastic wrap, then foil, and refrigerate at least 2 hours or up to 24 hours. Cut into 8 wedges to serve.

EACH SERVING About 390 calories | 19 g protein | 26 g carbohydrate | 24 g total fat (8 g saturated) | 44 mg cholesterol | 1,515 mg sodium.

GH Test Kitchen Tip

The sandwich tastes even better when made a day ahead.

Chicken Caesar Pockets

A sandwich and a salad rolled into one, these pockets make great picnic fare. Of course, you can always skip the pita and serve the salad on its own.

PREP 20 minutes   **COOK** about 12 minutes   **MAKES** 6 sandwiches

¼ **teaspoon salt**

2 **teaspoons plus 3 tablespoons olive oil**

½ **teaspoon coarsely ground black pepper**

4 **medium skinless, boneless chicken-breast halves (about 1 pound)**

3 **tablespoons lemon juice**

3 **tablespoons light mayonnaise**

1 **tablespoon Dijon mustard**

1 **teaspoon anchovy paste**

1 **small garlic clove, crushed with garlic press**

½ **cup grated Parmesan cheese**

6 **pitas (6- to 7-inch-diameter)**

8 **cups sliced Romaine lettuce (about 12-ounce head)**

1. Preheat broiler. In medium bowl, mix salt, 2 teaspoons olive oil, and ¼ teaspoon pepper.

Add chicken and stir to coat. Place chicken on rack in broiling pan. Place pan in broiler at closest position to source of heat; broil chicken about 12 minutes, turning once, until juices run clear when thickest part is pierced with tip of knife. Transfer chicken to cutting board; cool 5 minutes or until chicken is easy to handle.

2. Meanwhile, in large bowl, with fork, mix lemon juice, mayonnaise, mustard, anchovy paste, garlic, remaining 3 tablespoons olive oil, and ¼ teaspoon pepper until blended; stir in Parmesan cheese.

3. With sharp knife, slit top third of each pita to form an opening. Thinly slice chicken. Add lettuce and chicken slices to dressing; toss well to coat. Fill pitas with salad.

EACH SANDWICH About 345 calories | 17 g protein | 39 g carbohydrate | 13 g total fat (3 g saturated) | 26 mg cholesterol | 770 mg sodium.

Smoked Turkey and Mango Wraps

A sandwich of delightful counterpoints: luscious fresh mango—underscored by mango chutney—played against the rich meatiness of smoked turkey. The sandwich components are wrapped in lahvash, the soft version of Armenian cracker bread that ranges from 9 to 16 inches in diameter. Its thin texture is especially good with creamy spreads, like goat cheese or guacamole. If you can't find lahvash, divide filling ingredients among four 8- to 10-inch flour tortillas.

PREP 25 minutes plus chilling   **MAKES** 4 sandwiches

I large lime

¼ cup light mayonnaise

3 tablespoons mango chutney, chopped

½ teaspoon curry powder

⅛ teaspoon paprika

I lahvash (half 14-ounce package soft Armenian flatbread) (see Tip)

I medium cucumber, peeled and thinly sliced

8 ounces thinly sliced smoked turkey breast

I medium mango, peeled and finely chopped

6 large green-leaf lettuce leaves

1. Grate ¼ teaspoon peel and squeeze 1 tablespoon juice from lime. In small bowl, mix lime peel, lime juice, mayonnaise, chutney, curry, and paprika.

2. Unfold lahvash; spread with mayonnaise mixture. Top with cucumber slices, smoked turkey, chopped mango, and lettuce. Roll lahvash jelly-roll fashion.

3. Wrap lahvash roll in plastic and refrigerate 2 to 4 hours to allow bread to soften and flavor to develop.

4. To serve, trim ends, then cut lahvash roll into 4 pieces.

EACH SANDWICH About 280 calories | 18 g protein | 51 g carbohydrate | 2 g total fat (0 g saturated) | 23 mg cholesterol | 860 mg sodium.

GH Test Kitchen Tip

If lahvash seems dry before filling, place between dampened paper towels 10 to 15 minutes to soften.

Spicy Guacamole and Chicken Roll-Ups

Chock-full of chicken and served warm, this hearty sandwich is sure to please. The zesty guacamole tastes great with tortilla chips, too.

PREP 30 minutes   **COOK** about 12 minutes   **MAKES** 4 sandwiches

2 teaspoons olive oil

4 medium skinless, boneless chicken-breast halves (about 1 pound)

½ teaspoon salt

½ teaspoon coarsely ground black pepper

2 medium avocados (about 8 ounces each), peeled and cut into small chunks

1 medium tomato, diced

¼ cup loosely packed fresh cilantro leaves, coarsely chopped

4 teaspoons fresh lime juice

2 teaspoons finely chopped red onion

1 teaspoon adobo sauce from canned chipotle chiles (see Tip) or 2 tablespoons green jalapeño sauce

4 burrito-size (10-inch-diameter) flour tortillas, warmed

2 cups sliced iceberg lettuce

1. In 10-inch skillet, heat olive oil over medium-high heat until hot. Add chicken and sprinkle with ¼ teaspoon salt and ¼ teaspoon pepper. Cook chicken about 12 minutes, turning once, until juices run clear when thickest part is pierced with tip of knife. Transfer chicken to plate; cool 5 minutes or until easy to handle.

2. Meanwhile, in medium bowl, with rubber spatula, gently stir avocados, tomato, cilantro, lime juice, red onion, adobo sauce, and remaining ¼ teaspoon salt and ¼ teaspoon pepper until blended.

3. Pull chicken into thin shreds. Place tortillas on work surface; spread with guacamole. Place chicken, then lettuce on top of guacamole. Roll tortillas around filling.

EACH SANDWICH About 510 calories | 34 g protein | 40 g carbohydrate | 25 g total fat (4 g saturated) | 72 mg cholesterol | 625 mg sodium.

GH Test Kitchen Tip

Canned chipotle chiles in adobo (smoked jalapeño chiles in a vinegary marinade) are available in Hispanic markets and some large supermarkets.

Cajun Chicken Salad with Green Grapes

Enjoy a great combination of poached chicken, red pepper, and juicy grapes in a spicy, creamy dressing. We toasted the thyme and paprika to add extra flavor to the dressing and used reduced-fat sour cream to lower the fat.

PREP 25 minutes   **COOK** 20 minutes   **MAKES** 8 main-dish servings

1 lemon, thinly sliced

1 bay leaf

½ teaspoon whole black peppercorns

½ teaspoon dried thyme

6 medium skinless, boneless chicken-breast halves (1¾ pounds)

¾ teaspoon paprika

⅓ cup light mayonnaise

⅓ cup reduced-fat sour cream

¾ teaspoon salt

¼ teaspoon coarsely ground black pepper

⅛ teaspoon ground nutmeg

3 cups green grapes (about 12 ounces), each cut in half

1 large red pepper, cut into ½-inch dice

½ cup loosely packed fresh parsley leaves, chopped

¼ cup thinly sliced red onion

1 large pickled jalapeño chile, minced

1. In 12-inch skillet, heat *1 inch water* with lemon slices, bay leaf, peppercorns, and ¼ teaspoon thyme to boiling over high heat. Add chicken; reduce heat to low and simmer 12 to 14 minutes, turning chicken over halfway through cooking, until chicken just loses its pink color throughout. With slotted spoon or tongs, transfer chicken from skillet to cutting board; cool slightly until easy to handle. Cut chicken into ¾-inch pieces.

2. Discard poaching liquid and wipe skillet dry. Add paprika and remaining ¼ teaspoon thyme to skillet; toast over medium-low heat, stirring, 2 minutes.

3. Transfer paprika mixture to large bowl; stir in mayonnaise, sour cream, salt, pepper, and nutmeg until blended. Add chicken, grapes, red pepper, parsley, onion, and jalapeño; toss until evenly coated. Serve salad warm, or cover and refrigerate until ready to serve.

EACH SERVING About 200 calories | 24 g protein | 16 g carbohydrate | 4 g total fat (1 g saturated) | 64 mg cholesterol | 380 mg sodium.

Southwestern Turkey Fajitas

Broiling the tomatillos adds a subtle smokiness to this luscious salsa. Serve any extra salsa with tortilla chips.

PREP 30 minutes   BROIL about 20 minutes   MAKES 6 main-dish servings

TOMATILLO SALSA

1 pound tomatillos, husked and rinsed

1 small poblano chile, cut in half, stems and seeds discarded

1 small shallot, cut up

3 tablespoons fresh lime juice

¾ teaspoon salt

¾ teaspoon sugar

⅓ cup packed fresh cilantro leaves, chopped

TURKEY AND ONION FAJITAS

2 whole turkey-breast tenderloins (about 1¾ pounds) or 6 medium skinless, boneless chicken-breast halves (about 1¾ pounds)

2 tablespoons fajita seasoning (see Tip)

4 teaspoons olive oil

3 large onions, cut into ½-inch-thick slices

12 corn tortillas (6-inch)

cilantro sprigs and red chiles for garnish

1. Prepare Tomatillo Salsa: Preheat broiler. Place tomatillos in broiling pan without rack. Place pan in broiler 5 to 6 inches from source of heat and broil tomatillos 10 minutes or until blackened in spots and blistering, turning tomatillos over once. When tomatillos are turned, add poblano, skin side up, to pan and broil 6 minutes or until charred.

2. In blender or food processor with knife blade attached, pulse tomatillos, poblano, shallot, lime juice, salt, and sugar until chopped. Stir in cilantro; cover and refrigerate salsa up to 3 days if not serving right away. (Makes about 2 cups.)

3. Prepare Turkey and Onion Fajitas: In medium bowl, toss turkey tenderloins or chicken with fajita seasoning and 2 teaspoons oil. Brush onion slices with remaining 2 teaspoons oil.

4. Place turkey or chicken and onions on hot broiler pan rack. Cook the turkey 15 to 20 minutes (chicken 10 to 12 minutes) or until juices run clear when thickest part is pierced with tip of knife (internal temperature of turkey tenderloins should be 170° F on meat thermometer), turning turkey or chicken over once. Cook the onion slices 12 to 15 minutes or until tender and golden, turning them over once.

5. While turkey or chicken is cooking, place several tortillas on same broiler rack and heat just until lightly browned, removing tortillas to a sheet of foil as they brown. Wrap the tortillas in foil and keep warm.

6. To assemble Fajitas: Transfer onions to bowl. Transfer turkey or chicken to cutting board and thinly slice. Top tortillas with equal amounts of turkey or chicken and onion; spoon some salsa on each and fold over to eat out of hand. Garnish with cilantro sprigs and red chiles. Serve with any remaining onions and salsa.

EACH SERVING WITHOUT SALSA About 350 calories | 36 g protein | 35 g carbohydrate | 7 g total fat (I g saturated) | 88 mg cholesterol | 440 mg sodium.

EACH ¹/₄ CUP SALSA About 30 calories | I g protein | 6 g carbohydrate | I g total fat (0 g saturated) | 0 mg cholesterol | 220 mg sodium.

GH Test Kitchen Tip

Seasoning mixes vary among manufacturers, especially with regard to salt content. Add salt to taste if necessary.

Warm Chicken and Spinach Salad

A perfect dinner on the lighter side—sautéed chicken tenders and asparagus served on a bed of baby spinach, drizzled with mustard vinaigrette.

PREP 15 minutes   **COOK** 20 minutes   **MAKES** 4 main-dish servings

1 bag (about 6 ounces) baby spinach

3 teaspoons plus 1 tablespoon olive oil

1 pound medium asparagus, trimmed and cut diagonally into 1½-inch pieces

1 large shallot, thinly sliced

1 pound chicken-breast tenders

½ teaspoon salt

¼ teaspoon coarsely ground black pepper

1 tablespoon balsamic vinegar

1 tablespoon fresh lemon juice

½ teaspoon Dijon mustard

¼ teaspoon sugar

1. Place spinach leaves on large platter and set aside.

2. In nonstick 12-inch skillet, heat 2 teaspoons olive oil over medium-high heat until hot. Add asparagus and shallot, and cook 5 minutes or until golden, stirring occasionally. Reduce heat to medium; add *2 tablespoons water* and cook, covered, 5 minutes longer or until asparagus is tender, stirring occasionally. Spoon asparagus mixture over spinach.

3. Increase heat to medium-high. In same skillet, in 1 teaspoon olive oil, cook chicken with ¼ teaspoon salt and ⅛ teaspoon pepper until it loses its pink color throughout, 5 minutes, turning once.

4. Meanwhile, prepare dressing: In cup, with wire whisk or fork, mix vinegar, lemon juice, mustard, sugar, remaining 1 tablespoon olive oil, remaining ¼ teaspoon salt, and remaining ⅛ teaspoon pepper until blended.

5. Spoon chicken onto platter with spinach and asparagus. Add dressing to hot skillet and cook 30 seconds, stirring. Drizzle mixture over chicken and vegetables.

EACH SERVING About 225 calories | 30 g protein | 8 g carbohydrate | 9 g total fat (1 g saturated) | 66 mg cholesterol | 395 mg sodium.

Thai Salad

A summery blend of chicken, lettuce, fresh herbs, and crisp carrots tossed with a tangy, spicy Asian dressing. It is equally good made with either beef or shrimp in place of the chicken.

PREP 20 minutes   **MAKES** 4 main-dish servings

12 cups loosely packed bite-size pieces Boston lettuce (about two 6-ounce heads)

½ cup loosely packed fresh cilantro leaves

½ cup loosely packed fresh mint leaves

1 bag (10 ounces) shredded carrots

3 green onions, cut into 1-inch pieces

¼ cup fresh lime juice

2 tablespoons Asian fish sauce (see **Tip**, page 85)

2 tablespoons vegetable oil

1 jalapeño chile, seeded and minced

1 tablespoon grated, peeled fresh ginger

1 teaspoon sugar

12 ounces skinless, boneless, rotisserie chicken, cut into thin strips

1. In large bowl, toss lettuce with cilantro, mint, carrots, and green onions.

2. In another large bowl, with wire whisk, mix lime juice, fish sauce, oil, jalapeño, ginger, and sugar until blended.

3. To serve, add chicken to dressing in bowl; toss to coat. Add lettuce mixture; toss again.

EACH SERVING About 285 calories | 27 g protein | 14 g carbohydrate | 14 g total fat (2 g saturated) | 76 mg cholesterol | 755 mg sodium.

Curried Chicken and Mango Salad

Precooked chicken from the deli or supermarket makes our salad a cinch. The recipe can easily be doubled if you need to feed a crowd.

PREP **20 minutes**   MAKES **4 main-dish servings**

1 **store-bought rotisserie chicken (about 2 pounds)**

¼ **cup plain low-fat yogurt**

¼ **cup light mayonnaise**

2 **tablespoons mango chutney, chopped**

1 **tablespoon fresh lime juice**

1 **teaspoon curry powder**

1 **ripe large mango, peeled and diced**

1 **medium stalk celery, diced**

1 **medium Granny Smith apple, cored and diced**

½ **cup loosely packed fresh cilantro leaves, chopped**

1 **head leaf lettuce, separated and rinsed**

cilantro leaves for garnish

1. Remove skin from chicken; discard. With fingers, pull chicken meat into 1-inch pieces. (You should have about 3 cups, or about ¾ pound meat.)

2. In large bowl, mix yogurt, mayonnaise, chutney, lime juice, and curry powder until combined. Stir in chicken, mango, celery, apple, and cilantro until well coated. Serve salad on bed of lettuce leaves. Garnish with cilantro leaves.

EACH SERVING **About 310 calories** | **32 g protein** | **25 g carbohydrate** | **9 g total fat** (2 g saturated) | **95 mg cholesterol** | **255 mg sodium.**

Couscous and Smoked-Turkey Salad

Sweet nectarines contrast nicely with the smoky flavor of the turkey in this superquick salad. If you see plums, peaches, or apricots at the farmers' market, try using them in place of the nectarines.

PREP 10 minutes   COOK 5 minutes   MAKES 6 main-dish servings

1 teaspoon ground cumin

1 package (10 ounces) couscous (Moroccan pasta)

⅓ cup dried tart cherries

3 tablespoons fresh lemon juice

2 tablespoons olive oil

1 tablespoon Dijon mustard

¾ teaspoon salt

¼ teaspoon coarsely ground black pepper

3 ripe medium nectarines, diced

4 ounces smoked turkey breast (in 1 piece), cut into ¼-inch pieces

Boston lettuce leaves

1. In 3-quart saucepan, heat cumin over medium-high heat until fragrant, 1 to 3 minutes. In saucepan with cumin, prepare couscous as label directs, adding cherries but no salt or butter.

2. In large bowl, with wire whisk or fork, mix lemon juice, olive oil, mustard, salt, and pepper until dressing is blended.

3. Toss warm couscous mixture, diced nectarines, and turkey with dressing.

4. Spoon couscous onto large platter lined with Boston lettuce leaves.

EACH SERVING About 300 calories | 11 g protein | 51 g carbohydrate | 6 g total fat (1 g saturated) | 3 mg cholesterol | 470 mg sodium.

Best Tuna Salad

You can enjoy this simple family favorite two ways—on a sandwich or on a bed of salad greens. For a change of pace, try one of our three tasty new variations.

PREP 15 minutes   MAKES 1¼ cups or 2 main-dish servings

1 can (6 ounces) chunk-light tuna packed in water, drained

¼ cup finely chopped celery

3 tablespoons light mayonnaise

2 teaspoons fresh lemon juice

baguette or other favorite bread (optional)

In small bowl, with fork, combine all ingredients except baguette. Cover and refrigerate if not serving right away. Serve on a baguette if you like.

EACH SERVING WITHOUT BREAD About 170 calories | 19 g protein | 1 g carbohydrate | 11 g total fat (3 g saturated) | 30 mg cholesterol | 415 mg sodium.

CURRIED TUNA Prepare Best Tuna Salad as above. Stir in ½ **cup finely chopped Granny Smith apple** and **1 teaspoon curry powder**. Serve on raisin-walnut or sourdough bread if you like. Makes about 1½ cups or 2 main-dish servings.

EACH SERVING WITHOUT BREAD About 190 calories | 20 g protein | 7 g carbohydrate | 11 g total fat (3 g saturated) | 30 mg cholesterol | 415 mg sodium.

MEDITERRANEAN TUNA Prepare Best Tuna Salad as above. Stir in **2 tablespoons capers**, chopped, and ¼ **teaspoon freshly grated lemon peel**. Serve on Italian bread if you like. Makes about 1¼ cups or 2 main-dish servings.

EACH SERVING WITHOUT BREAD About 170 calories | 19 g protein | 2 g carbohydrate | 11 g total fat (3 g saturated) | 30 mg cholesterol | 730 mg sodium.

SOUTHWESTERN TUNA Prepare Best Tuna Salad as above. Stir in **2 tablespoons chopped fresh cilantro leaves** and **1 pickled jalapeño chile**, finely chopped. Serve rolled up in warm flour tortillas if you like. Makes about 1¼ cups or 2 main-dish servings.

EACH SERVING WITHOUT TORTILLA About 170 calories | 19 g protein | 2 g carbohydrate | 11 g total fat (3 g saturated) | 30 mg cholesterol | 510 mg sodium.

Tuscan Tuna on Focaccia

This filling also tastes great served in pita pockets. Be sure to rinse the cannellini beans—it removes some of the sodium.

PREP 15 minutes **MAKES** 4 sandwiches

1 can (16 to 19 ounces) white kidney beans (cannellini), rinsed and drained

½ cup chopped fresh basil leaves

3 tablespoons capers, chopped

2 tablespoons fresh lemon juice

2 tablespoons olive oil

½ teaspoon salt

¼ teaspoon ground black pepper

1 can (6 ounces) tuna packed in water, drained

1 bunch watercress, trimmed

1 round or square (8-inch) focaccia bread, cut horizontally in half

2 ripe tomatoes, thinly sliced

1. In large bowl, mash 1 cup kidney beans. Stir in basil, capers, lemon juice, olive oil, salt, and pepper. Add tuna, watercress, and remaining beans; toss well.

2. Spoon tuna mixture on the bottom half of focaccia; top with tomato slices. Replace top of focaccia.

EACH SANDWICH About 490 calories | 32 g protein | 65 g carbohydrate | 13 g total fat (1 g saturated) | 7 mg cholesterol | 1,455 mg sodium.

Niçoise Salad

As the story goes, the first Niçoise salad was created in eighteenth-century France, and it's been a hit ever since.

PREP 35 minutes   **COOK** 25 minutes   **MAKES** 4 main-dish servings

1 tablespoon white wine vinegar

1 tablespoon fresh lemon juice

1 tablespoon minced shallot

1 teaspoon Dijon mustard

1 teaspoon anchovy paste

¼ teaspoon sugar

¼ teaspoon coarsely ground black pepper

3 tablespoons extravirgin olive oil

1 pound medium red potatoes, not peeled, cut into ¼-inch-thick slices

8 ounces French green beans (haricots verts) or regular green beans, trimmed

1 head Boston lettuce, leaves separated

12 cherry tomatoes, each cut in half

1 can (12 ounces) solid white tuna packed in water, drained and flaked

2 large hard-cooked eggs, peeled and each cut into quarters

½ cup Niçoise olives

1. Prepare dressing: In small bowl, with wire whisk, mix vinegar, lemon juice, shallot, mustard, anchovy paste, sugar, and pepper until blended. In thin, steady stream, whisk in oil until blended.

2. In 3-quart saucepan, combine potatoes and *enough water to cover*; heat to boiling over high heat. Reduce heat; cover and simmer until tender, about 10 minutes. Drain.

3. Meanwhile, in 10-inch skillet, heat *1 inch water* to boiling over high heat. Add green beans; heat to boiling. Reduce heat to low and cook until tender-crisp, 6 to 8 minutes. Drain; rinse with cold running water. Drain.

4. To serve, pour half of dressing into medium bowl. Add lettuce leaves and toss to coat. Line large platter with dressed lettuce leaves. Arrange potatoes, green beans, cherry tomatoes, tuna, hard-cooked eggs, and olives in separate piles on lettuce. Drizzle remaining dressing over salad.

EACH SERVING About 440 calories | 30 g protein | 30 g carbohydrate | 23 g total fat (4 g saturated) | 140 mg cholesterol | 716 mg sodium.

> ### GH Test Kitchen Tip
> Haricots verts are very thin, delicately flavored green beans. Look for fresh crisp beans with a bright color.

Old-Time Tomato Sandwiches

When tomatoes are at their peak, all you need is good crusty bread and a little mayo to make a heavenly sandwich. A little watercress tucked inside makes a nice addition.

PREP 15 minutes   **MAKES** 4 sandwiches

1 lemon

⅓ cup mayonnaise

¼ teaspoon ground coriander

¼ teaspoon salt

¼ teaspoon coarsely ground black pepper

1 large round or oval loaf (1 pound) sourdough or other crusty bread

3 ripe large tomatoes, thickly sliced

1. From lemon, grate ½ teaspoon peel and squeeze 1 teaspoon juice. In small bowl, stir lemon peel and juice, mayonnaise, coriander, salt, and pepper.

2. Cut eight ½-inch-thick slices from center of bread loaf. Reserve ends for use another day. Toast bread if desired. Spread 1 side of each bread slice with mayonnaise mixture. Arrange tomato slices on 4 bread slices; top with remaining bread slices, mayonnaise side down. Cut each sandwich in half to serve.

EACH SANDWICH About 300 calories | 6 g protein | 35 g carbohydrate | 18 g total fat (3 g saturated) | 7 mg cholesterol | 540 mg sodium.

Frittata Sandwiches with Peppers and Onions

This hot sandwich can be wrapped in foil and carried along to serve later—perfect for potlucks and meals on the run.

PREP 30 minutes   BAKE 10 minutes   MAKES 4 sandwiches

2 tablespoons olive oil

2 medium onions, each cut in half and thinly sliced

4 Italian frying peppers (about 2 ounces each), thinly sliced

1/2 teaspoon salt

6 large eggs

3/4 cup grated Parmesan cheese

1/4 cup chopped fresh parsley leaves

1/4 teaspoon ground black pepper

1 round or square (8-inch) focaccia bread, cut horizontally in half

1. In 12-inch skillet, heat 1 tablespoon olive oil over medium heat. Add onions and cook, stirring frequently, until tender, about 8 minutes. Add Italian peppers; sprinkle with 1/4 teaspoon salt and cook until peppers are tender, about 12 minutes longer. Keep warm.

2. Meanwhile, preheat oven to 375°F. In large bowl, with wire whisk or fork, mix eggs, Parmesan, parsley, black pepper, and remaining 1/4 teaspoon salt until blended. In nonstick 10-inch skillet with oven-safe handle, heat remaining 1 tablespoon olive oil over medium heat. Pour in egg mixture and cook without stirring, 3 to 4 minutes, until frittata begins to set around the edge.

3. Place skillet in oven. Bake about 10 minutes longer or until frittata is just set and knife inserted in center comes out clean. Slide frittata onto plate.

4. Place frittata on the bottom half of focaccia; top with onion-pepper mixture. Replace top of focaccia.

EACH SANDWICH About 535 calories | 29 g protein | 49 g carbohydrate | 26 g total fat (7 g saturated) | 341 mg cholesterol | 1,225 mg sodium.

Portobello Burgers

We marinate the "burgers" in a broth mixture accented with thyme to add extra flavor, then serve them up on buns with a lemony mayonnaise.

PREP 15 minutes plus marinating   **COOK** 16 to 20 minutes   **MAKES** 4 sandwiches

¼ **cup chicken broth**

2 **tablespoons olive oil**

2 **teaspoons balsamic vinegar**

1 **teaspoon fresh thyme leaves**

¼ **teaspoon salt**

¼ **teaspoon coarsely ground black pepper**

4 **medium (about 4-inch-diameter) Portobello mushrooms, stems discarded**

1 **lemon**

⅓ **cup mayonnaise**

1 **small green onion, minced**

4 **large (about 4-inch-diameter) buns**

1 **bunch arugula**

1. In glass baking dish just large enough to hold mushrooms in a single layer, mix chicken broth, olive oil, vinegar, thyme, ⅛ teaspoon salt, and ⅛ teaspoon pepper. Add mushrooms, turning to coat. Let stand 30 minutes, turning occasionally.

2. Meanwhile, from lemon, grate ½ teaspoon peel and squeeze ½ teaspoon juice. In small bowl, stir lemon peel, lemon juice, mayonnaise, green onion, remaining ⅛ teaspoon salt, and remaining ⅛ teaspoon pepper.

3. Prepare outdoor grill or heat 10-inch grill pan over medium heat until hot. Add mushrooms and cook about 8 to 10 minutes per side, turning occasionally and brushing with remaining marinade, until mushrooms are browned and cooked through.

4. Cut each bun horizontally in half. Spread cut sides of buns with mayonnaise mixture; top with arugula leaves. Place warm grilled mushrooms on bottom halves of buns; replace top half of buns to serve.

EACH SANDWICH About 355 calories | 6 g protein | 30 g carbohydrate | 25 g total fat (4 g saturated) | 7 mg cholesterol | 585 mg sodium.

Vegetarian Black-Bean Burritos

A deceptively rich and tasty combination of fat-free bean chili, rice, fresh corn, and spicy cheese—all wrapped up in warm flour tortillas.

PREP 10 minutes COOK 15 minutes MAKES 4 main-dish servings

½ cup regular long-grain rice

4 low-fat flour tortillas (10-inch diameter)

1¼ cups fresh corn kernels (about 2 large ears corn)

1 can (15 ounces) spicy fat-free black-bean chili

1 can (8 ounces) tomato sauce

¼ cup shredded Monterey Jack cheese with jalapeño chiles (1 ounce)

⅓ cup packed fresh cilantro leaves, chopped

1. Preheat oven to 300°F. In 2-quart saucepan, prepare rice as label directs but do not add salt or butter or margarine.

2. Meanwhile, wrap tortillas in foil; heat in oven until warm, about 15 minutes.

3. When rice is done, stir in corn, black-bean chili, and tomato sauce. Heat to boiling over medium-high heat; boil 1 minute.

4. Spoon about 1 cup chili mixture down center of each tortilla; sprinkle with cheese and cilantro. Fold sides of tortillas over filling. Place burritos seam side down on platter.

EACH SERVING About 430 calories | 15 g protein | 75 g carbohydrate | 8 g total fat (2 g saturated) | 8 mg cholesterol | 910 mg sodium.

Falafel Sandwiches

Serve these small bean patties in pita pockets with lettuce, tomatoes, and cucumbers. For a tangy finishing touch, spoon in a little plain yogurt.

PREP 10 minutes   **COOK** 8 minutes per batch   **MAKES** 4 sandwiches

4 green onions, cut into 1-inch pieces

2 garlic cloves, each cut in half

½ cup packed fresh Italian parsley leaves

2 teaspoons dried mint

1 can (15 to 19 ounces) garbanzo beans, rinsed and drained

½ cup plain dried bread crumbs

1 teaspoon ground coriander

1 teaspoon ground cumin

1 teaspoon baking powder

½ teaspoon salt

¼ teaspoon ground red pepper (cayenne)

¼ teaspoon ground allspice

olive oil nonstick cooking spray

4 pitas (6- to 7-inch diameter)

accompaniments: sliced romaine lettuce, sliced tomatoes, sliced cucumber, sliced red onion, plain low-fat yogurt

1. In food processor with knife blade attached, finely chop green onions, garlic, parsley, and mint. Add garbanzo beans, bread crumbs, coriander, cumin, baking powder, salt, ground red pepper, and allspice, and blend until a coarse puree forms.

2. Shape bean mixture, by scant ½ cups, into eight 3-inch round patties and place on sheet of waxed paper. Spray both sides of patties with olive oil spray.

3. Heat nonstick 10-inch skillet over medium-high heat until hot. Add half of patties and cook 8 minutes or until dark golden brown, turning once. Transfer the patties to paper towels to drain. Repeat with the remaining patties.

4. Cut off top third of each pita to form a pocket. Place warm patties in pitas. Serve with choice of accompaniments.

EACH SANDWICH WITHOUT ACCOMPANIMENTS About 365 calories | 14 g protein | 68 g carbohydrate | 5 g total fat (1 g saturated) | 0 mg cholesterol | 1,015 mg sodium.

Szechuan Peanut-Noodle Salad

Cold sesame noodles, a popular offering in Chinese restaurants, are the inspiration for this flavor-packed pasta salad.

PREP 25 minutes   COOK 25 minutes   MAKES 5 main-dish or 8 accompaniment servings

1 package (16 ounces) linguine or spaghetti

2½ teaspoons salt

4 ounces snow peas, strings removed

½ cup creamy peanut butter

1 tablespoon grated, peeled fresh ginger

¼ cup soy sauce

2 tablespoons distilled white vinegar

2 teaspoons Asian sesame oil

¼ teaspoon hot pepper sauce

1 small cucumber (6 ounces), peeled, seeded, and cut into 2" by ¼" matchstick strips

¼ cup dry-roasted peanuts

1 green onion, chopped

1. In large saucepot, cook linguine as label directs, using 2 teaspoons salt.

2. Meanwhile, in 3-quart saucepan, combine *1 inch water* and snow peas; heat to boiling over high heat. Reduce heat and simmer 2 minutes; drain. Rinse with cold running water; drain. Cut snow peas lengthwise into ¼-inch-wide matchstick strips. Set aside.

3. Drain linguine, reserving *1 cup pasta water*. Prepare dressing: In large bowl, with wire whisk, mix peanut butter, ginger, reserved pasta water, soy sauce, vinegar, sesame oil, remaining ½ teaspoon salt, and hot pepper sauce until smooth.

4. Add linguine to dressing in bowl and toss to coat. Add snow peas and cucumber; toss to combine. Sprinkle with the peanuts and the green onion.

EACH MAIN-DISH SERVING About 572 calories | 22 g protein | 78 g carbohydrate | 20 g total fat (3 g saturated) | 0 mg cholesterol | 1,794 mg sodium.

GH Test Kitchen Tip

This salad can be made ahead and served cold. Prepare and chill separately the linguine, dressing, and vegetables. Toss together just before serving.

Index